OBJECTS:USA 2024

Kellie Riggs & Angelik Vizcarrondo-Laboy

Foreword by Zesty Meyers and Evan Snyderman

Introduction by Glenn Adamson

Edited by Mina Warchavchik Hugerth

August Editions

CONTENTS

ARTISTS

FOREWORD
ZESTY MEYERS AND EVAN SNYDERMAN

This publication and accompanying exhibition mark the second iteration of a longstanding goal R & Company has set out to achieve: to lead and set the standard for recognizing outstanding makers in America. With so much creativity and talent brewing in the country, we developed *Objects: USA* (borrowing its name from the seminal 1969 exhibition), initially as a survey and now a triennial, to capture the energy of the movements happening around us. *Objects: USA* offers an incisive exploration of the formal innovations and conceptual motivations that shape the distinct and varied landscape of today's object-making. As it progresses, this series will become a key reference for understanding creativity in America.

In recent years, collectible design has increasingly entered popular consciousness, partly thanks to the diversity of individuals embracing handmade processes and propelling them in new directions. Markers of identity have been translated into objects in ways that reflect large societal changes as much as deeply personal stories. Many talented artists have developed new ways of working with materials and styles that simply did not exist before, while others have reinvented traditional mediums to sustain their relevance. As tastes and trends continue to evolve, possibilities keep growing, but one constant has remained: the power of the human hand. Technology progressively offers us new tools with which we make things, but the yearning to touch and feel—taking a step back from our increasingly cybernated age—is as relevant as ever.

The shows and accompanying catalogs are guided by insightful guest curators who bring their points of view to the table and expand the conversation. Their mission is to scour the country and find the most exciting things being created today, selecting makers from various generations and origins. Whatever path these people took to be in the USA making objects today becomes a block in the astounding cultural patchwork that drives this country.

Our inaugural *Objects: USA* happened in 2020–21, guided by guest curators Glenn Adamson, Abby Bangser, and R & Company's James Zemaitis. For this second edition, Angelik Vizcarrondo-Laboy and Kellie Riggs have taken the reins, supported by Adamson as a curatorial advisor. Joining forces and distinct perspectives, the pair proposes a groundbreaking presentation of fifty-five makers born in twenty-three American states and abroad, all working in the USA with techniques as varied as their points of view. Together, the 2024 roster offers an exceptional showcase of design, craft, and art today and where it is heading, organized in a way that redefines how we think about object making.

The publication and exhibition are structured around concepts that engage with artists' intentions and driving interests—rather than traditional categories related to medium—allowing for a more vibrant examination of creative approaches, material explorations, and making processes. They are divided among broad conceptual categories defined by Vizcarrondo-Laboy and Riggs as "seven archetypes of objecthood." These include the Truthsayers, who honor the simple nature of their materials and emphasize slow, manual processes; the Betatesters, who engage in material subversion and innovation in a post-digital landscape; the

Doomsdayers, who work with an array of materials and processes to create works fit for future civilizations while revisiting past and present; the Insiders, who celebrate and subvert our relationships with the domestic realm; the Mediators, who focus on identity, environment, and the interactions between person, space, and object; the Codebreakers, who make modular or coded objects as conceptual puzzles; and the Keepers, who explore narrative storytelling, history, memory, and connection in its various permutations. Together, the works in *Objects: USA 2024* engage audiences with an overview of contemporary making that is distinctly of the moment and part of a lasting historical trajectory.

By documenting what is happening in the interconnected territories of design, craft, and art in the United States today, R & Company aims to amplify the voices of those shaping our cultural narrative. While this edition is on view at our gallery, the 2020 exhibition tours the country, fulfilling our vision to redefine collaboration, transcend traditional roles, and foster new strategies to uplift artists and propel society forward. We know the desire to make things is inherent to human nature, and we believe this exhibition and subsequent ones will enhance our sense of self and our understanding of each other.

We thank everyone who contributed their time, ideas, opinions, and care to this project. We could not have done it without you all.

Welcome to *Objects: USA 2024*.

Do me a favor. Before reading this introduction, flip through the book—if you haven't already—taking in the extraordinary assemblage of objects it contains. Then come on back.

. . . Amazing, right? Every one of the works featured in these pages is an indelible emblem of The Now. Individually, they manifest extraordinary material intelligence. Aesthetic invention. Associative thinking. Collectively, they make up a terrain of extraordinary extent and diversity. To summarize it all would be impossible. Even providing a basic map by which to navigate it is quite difficult—but not impossible, for that's precisely what this catalog sets out to do.

First, a little backstory. Fifty-five years ago, *Objects: USA*—curated by art dealer Lee Nordness and director of the Museum of Contemporary Crafts (now the Museum of Arts and Design) Paul J. Smith—opened in Washington, DC. The exhibition proceeded to tour for several years thereafter and, together with its accompanying catalog, swiftly attained something like biblical status. The project documented the full scope of American craft like nothing before or since, establishing the catechism of clay, fiber, glass, metal, and wood that would organize the movement's sense of itself for decades (it also had small categories for enamels, mosaic, and plastics). What's more, it did so when the movement was at its height, both creatively speaking and in terms of its cultural relevance.

About half a century later, in 2020, I led the curatorial team for a reprise presented at R & Company, together with Abby Bangser and the gallery team of Zesty Meyers, Evan Snyderman, and James Zemaitis. We selected fifty artists who had participated in the original show and set alongside them works by fifty of today's most compelling makers. This exhibition, too, is now traveling to museums across America.

It's a success story, without a doubt. Yet the question of what, exactly, is being surveyed has been a part of *Objects: USA* from the start. Nordness, in his essay for the original catalog, revealed his preoccupations with art status. "Can a chair ever be a work of art? Can a teapot?" he asked. Then answered, "Let each creative person decide if he be an artist or a craftsman; let critics and collectors and museum professionals decide if he be a good or a bad artist." That question hovered over the exhibition everywhere it went, with virtually every press response asking whether—and if so, how—the works in the show had transcended craft and become something more.

In preparing the 2020 edition, we adopted a different perspective, arguing that craft, far from being a condition to escape, was in fact a pervasive and potent force, a necessary aspect of almost any successful work of contemporary art or design. This left us with an apparent dilemma: how would we decide what to include? In practice, this was no problem. By adopting the first *Objects: USA* as our explicit model, we gave ourselves an outline to curate into. Though we abandoned the original show's materials-based organizing principle, we did emphasize those areas in our selection. Stylistically and conceptually, too, present-day practitioners were chosen for their evident resonance with the previous generation. Idioms that were at their height in the late 1960s, like Funk ceramics and monumental fiber art, found obvious

This page and the next: Installation views of the original *Objects: USA* show at the Smithsonian American Art Museum, 1969 (top), and installation views of *Objects: USA 2020* at R & Company, 2021 (bottom)

correspondences on the contemporary side of the show.

No such armature for *Objects: USA 2024*. Its talented curators Angelik Vizcarrondo-Laboy and Kellie Riggs have launched themselves into free space. A historical foundation is still evident in this new edition, not least through the inclusion of several widely recognized veterans in the roster of artists. But Vizcarrondo-Laboy and Riggs have been so bold as to establish a new categorical structure, which amounts to nothing less than a hypothetical framework for understanding twenty-first-century objecthood. The works they've gathered are by turns earnest, experimental, and apocalyptic—a reflection of the state of things today—and their curation of this material itself feels like a form of art, or perhaps concrete poetry. Their inventive classification draws out unexpected connections that accumulate gradually into a conceptual matrix.

At the end of his essay for *Objects: USA*, Nordness commented, "It now seems a miracle that these artists persisted, despite their isolation not only from the public but from each other." What had kept the studio craft movement going, he believed, was the combination of "emotional-intellectual involvement" that only a handmade thing can offer: "The one-of-a-kind object is inherently personal, the rapport intimate." Much has changed since he wrote those words. The dynamic today seems almost opposite, in fact: the prospect of isolation is remote, thanks to the networks propagated, in no small part, by the craft movement itself. A wellspring of solidarity now crosses over all disciplinary and aesthetic distinctions. On the negative side, constant hyper-connectedness threatens to overwhelm individual creative vision, drowning it in a tide of the merely interesting.

One thing, however, remains the same. The intimacy of objects, the way they combine the emotional and the intellectual, still animates the imagination of countless artists. And the things they make help us to situate ourselves in time, space, and culture. To seize this possibility, we need to situate them in turn. This is what Vizcarrondo-Laboy and Riggs have done: surveyed the vast complex of making today and proposed a way to see in it a shape, manifold, beguiling, and provocative. The next time *Objects: USA* rolls around, in three years, it will all be different. But they have given us a way to grasp what's actually happening out there. Read further, now—and hold on tight.

OBJECTS: USA 2024: SEVEN ARCHETYPES OF OBJECTHOOD
KELLIE RIGGS AND ANGELIK VIZCARRONDO-LABOY

Humans are uniquely devoted to the creation, reproduction, and reinvention of objects. We depend on them to fulfill our needs and desires. We want to possess and collect them. We care about what they look like and what they are made of. And most of all, we are invested in the motivation behind their creation and the personal, cultural, and political meanings we imbue within them. These fundamental truths form the conceptual framework of *Objects: USA 2024*.

This project, an exhibition and catalog and the second edition of R & Company's *Objects: USA* triennial, is a survey of work by fifty-five artists, designers, and studios based in the United States. All redefine our perceptions of objecthood through a central tension between subversion and affirmation; they rearrange expectations of their chosen materials and formats, and question what it is an object gets to be. As a capsule of our moment in time, our curatorial focus is on living and practicing makers working across diverse mediums and styles. Many of them are shining, emerging voices in their respective fields, while others have a lifetime of achievement worth recognizing within this context, individually interpolating art, design, and craft with ease. Despite our attention to makers in the present tense, we know they do not work, nor do these objects exist, in a historical vacuum. We pay respect to the ancestors whose skills, vision, labor, and determination have shaped our understanding of the state of the object.

It is an impossible endeavor to capture the production of objects in the United States in its entirety with a finite number of examples, but we can outline how different it looks and feels from the inception of *Objects: USA* over half a century ago. Now more than ever, the intersectional classist, racist, and misogynistic hierarchies of the art world that once boxed in artists working in craft disciplines are dissolving. However, it is critical to note that despite the historical marginalization of craft artists, the field itself was not exempt from bias. While women were well represented in the 1969 *Objects: USA*—in vivid contrast to contemporaneous painting and sculpture—artists of color comprised less than 10 percent of the participants,[1] mirroring the dominance of white artists in the mid-century studio craft movement and the art world in general. The original exhibition took place in a time period defined by social movements for racial justice (notably, the civil rights movement, the Asian American movement, and the Chicano movement), and the art world is still catching up to the necessary changes. The unfolding developments also created a desire and expectation for objects to do more, be more—to be tangible containers of intangible concepts.

In the last five years, there has been significant progress in recognizing the historical and contemporary critical contributions of artists of color to their fields, who, without access to the same education and platforms as their white counterparts, were often relegated to the worlds of so-called outsider and folk art. For instance, although Native American artists have thrived within autonomous art spaces since before the mid-century, this does not excuse their problematic historical exclusion, especially in a contemporary sense, from American art institutions and galleries. We acknowledge that this includes previous iterations of *Objects: USA,* a particularly egregious omission that diminishes centuries of craft innovation and artistic expression in the handmade arts. While the 2024 version of *Objects: USA* is far more inclusive, we hope that future iterations will evolve to even more accurately reflect the kaleidoscope of people that make up the United States.

Through their commitment to reimagining and recontextualizing their chosen medium and format, artists working in these disciplines—especially those with politicized histories—have catalyzed the art world's embrace of craft. It's about time. From calls to represent the United States at the Venice Biennale (Simone Leigh and Jeffrey Gibson) to countless monographs, institutional retrospectives, solo exhibitions, and commercial success, the demand for these artists is at an all-time high. This is true for ceramic artists, and particularly so for those currently working in fiber. Works by Sharif Farrag, Raven Halfmoon, Diedrick Brackens, Bisa Butler, and Jeremy Frey, for example, are frequently spoken for before they are even made. We applaud that this is the case. This exciting momentum encourages makers working within craft-based formats to continue to develop their practices and share their distinctive perspectives—especially up-and-coming talent, which our roster bolsters.

With this in mind, we have placed the participants of *Objects: USA 2024* into a spectrum of generative categories, rather than more conventional medium-based or period-based sections. The names of our categories—Truthsayers, Betatesters, Doomsdayers, Insiders, Mediators, Codebreakers, and Keepers—reflect the intentionality and concerns of the makers. They are purposely active to provide invigorating routes to the core of each practice. We developed a similarly fluid structure for this catalog, presenting some artists within overlapping spaces. In this way, this exhibition functions as a foil to the 1969 *Objects: USA*, as well as its successor in 2020. However, as a tender nod to where it all began, we have included objects representing each of the nine materials spotlighted in the original exhibition: enamel, ceramic, glass, metals, jewelry, plastics, mosaics, wood, and fibers.

Conscious of cultural and political contexts of creation, the artists and designers in our cohort craft objects as markers of identity, byproducts of environmental tension, beacons of tradition, odes to materiality and process, symbols of protest, containers of feeling, future relics, and so much more. In this essay, we dive into each category by discussing the artists that helped to generate them, and what their objects suggest about how they see the world.

TRUTHSAYERS

In an age when the screens at our fingertips flood us with a steady stream of the next best things, there is a strain of faithful artists and designers who resist the urge to constantly reinvent. They are committed to slow processes; simple, carefully chosen materials; and meticulous, repetitious techniques. To encounter this work is to take a respite from the commotion of contemporary society; the objects are materialized pauses to wear, hold, or sit on. The kind of work included in the Truthsayers category is an honest reminder of the connection between the hand and the object. It is rooted in the tried and true, and within this exhibition catalog, provides an essential foundation for wilder things to come.

The Truthsayers celebrate the inherent qualities of natural materials, like the grain of wood and the veining of marble. It is a direct approach that seeks to accentuate rather than transform beyond recognition. This pursuit is crystal clear in the work of Nik Gelormino and Ian Collings, who pride themselves in animating chunks of wood and stone with the humble tools of the trade. In their hands, these hardy raw materials become creamy and sensuous. Together, Collings's unctuous sculptures are an earthy smorgasbord of travertine, marble, calcite, alabaster, onyx, or granite. He seldom combines types in a single work; instead he brings a focus to the hypnotizing patterning of each piece, which the artist carves and polishes into a singular seductive form. Gelormino's sweet stools are likewise genuine expressions of his reverence for nature. He gives locally sourced wood new purpose by leaving the marks of his chisel evident while showcasing the rings and scars that

memorialize the tree's past life. For both artists, the deliberate choice to work with natural materials is important; Collings says, "It's a way to seek a deeper connection. I embrace the animistic perspective of the world and honor that matter."[2]

Makers in this category like Minjae Kim and Lonnie Vigil honor traditional methodologies and, at times, culturally specific languages, while establishing their own distinctive points of view. Kim prefers the straightforwardness of classic joinery in his furniture while maintaining a modern sensibility. His sought-after "one-liners,"[3] as he calls them, might seem abstract but are explicit references to Korean aesthetics that the Western world has appropriated, and act as a means to reconnect with his heritage while navigating American culture. Due to his consistency and transparency of assemblage, what you see is what you get, even when using less-expected materials, like quilted and draped fiberglass. Unlike much of contemporary furniture design that prompts questions about use and broader definitions of purpose, Kim's chairs are uncomplicated, the rounded M-shaped carving at the seat inviting you to sit down. They embody a still certainty in their familiar utilitarian form.

Once a businessman who found no soul in business, Truthsayer Lonnie Vigil returned to Tewa land in New Mexico and began making Nambé pottery. This tradition of smooth, hand-coiled, unglazed vessels made of iron-rich micaceous clay had almost disappeared in the mid-twentieth century. Not only did Vigil put his stamp on this discipline from his Puebloan heritage, but he also revived the practice and

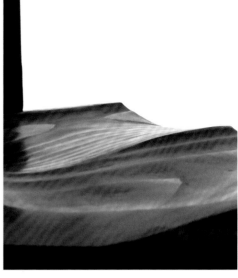

continues its legacy four decades later. Vigil is a contrasting but vital figure in the landscape of Indigenous pottery, where techniques are typically passed down generationally. Although his great-aunts and great-grandmother were potters, he is self-taught and initially resisted looking at his family's work to find his own formal language. In the Southwest, there are more than twenty Pueblo tribes, which are small and geographically close together, each producing pottery in a particular style. Vigil's minimal, undecorated forms stand apart from the more carved, graphic, or painterly surface applications famous in other Pueblos, and recontextualize a pottery practice intended for utilitarian purposes (see p. 58).

Vigil's vessels encapsulate material honesty, with surfaces that can be read like a book. In a series of videos where the potter handles antique jars, he says, "This piece obviously has carried a lot of water. I feel like I can tell that by the hand marks over time, the oil from the body . . . the hands have taken away the finish."[4] Although now highly collectible wares, Vigil's vessels can still be used for cooking. About the dark sheen on another pot, he says, "It's possible that it was fired on a cloudy day,"[5] because cloudy days often produce more smoke. These surface gradations on Vigil's ceramics serve as a record of the firing process, where "fire clouds"

Top left: Ian Collings. *Stone Seat Grooved - Red Travertine I*, 2023. Red travertine (detail)

Top right: Minjae Kim. *Gate Chair*, 2022. Stained Douglas fir (detail)

Left: Nik Gelormino. *Flat Car (no. 02)*, 2023. Fir (detail and full view on p. 46)

leave behind the soft black markings of carbon from ash that help identify and place his work.

Material wisdom and lack of pretension bring this group together. The Truthsayers' commitment to repetitive, diligent processes also reminds us that sometimes artists create simply for the joy of making. Basket weaving, the foundation for the decades-long practices of Mary Lee Hu and Ferne Jacobs, is paradigmatic among those processes. Hu, a jeweler, weaves, twines, and knots pure gold wire into regal wearable sculpture, a time-consuming activity she finds meditative. Seemingly more traditional yet highly experimental, Jacobs uses

natural fibers typically used for basketry, such as waxed linen, to coil organic freestanding or wall-mounted sculptures. Both Jacobs and Hu are artists whose timeless work represents a lingering urge to relentlessly come to know their chosen material and format.

Alternatively, Jamie Bennett has continuously found new ways to exploit the transformative properties of enamel. A delicate dance between glass dust, a hot kiln, and a soft but deliberate hand has allowed him to create colorful, painterly masterpieces for the body and in the round. He is the standout contemporary example of an artist embodying enamel as a verb and noun, who equally considers the front and back sides of his pieces. For instance, the reverse of brooch *Ravenna No. 9* (see p. 70) depicts a tongue-in-cheek list of its own raw and processed materials with their source locations to help future historians avoid speculation. "People zoom past things. Looking has changed dramatically within the last few generations. My work slows things down a little,"[6] he says. Bennett is one of only two representatives here for what was a whole (albeit small) category in the original *Objects: USA* exhibition.

With wood, stone, ceramic, fiber, enamel, and metal, the Truthsayers keep it uncomplicated, even if the processes are not easy or simple. When viewing them, we can take pleasure in seeing how these objects came to be. It is also unsurprising that some of our most seasoned artists are in this foundational category. They, like other renowned artists in the exhibition and many recognized in past iterations of *Objects: USA*, have given our younger makers the freedom to explore, break the rules, and rewrite them. Yet the category also features emerging artists who underscore that the approach discussed here is timeless. You are bound to reencounter the principles of the Truthsayers, on their own or remixed, time and time again.

Top: Ferne Jacobs. *Waves*, 2019. Waxed linen thread

Right: Mary Lee Hu. *Choker #83*, 2000. 18- and 22-karat gold. Tacoma Art Museum. Museum purchase with funds from the Rotasa Foundation and Susan Beech with additional contributions from the Art Jewelry Forum, Sharon Campbell, Lloyd E. Herman, Karen Lorene, Mia McEldowney, Mobilia Gallery, Flora Book, Ramona Solberg, Judy Wagonfeld, Nancy Worden, and the Ramona Solberg Endowment, 2006.10 (detail)

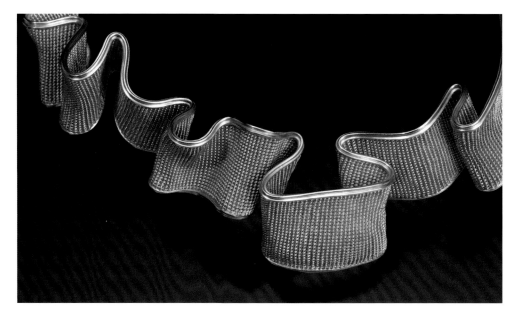

BETATESTERS

With relentless curiosity, the Betatesters push the physical possibilities of materials to the extreme by engaging in research and experimentation on the effects of new processes. In doing so, they often challenge the expectations of archetypal forms and formats found in art and design, as well as assumptions about sensory perception. Rather than be the antithesis of the Truthsayers, the Betatesters reveal many an answer to the age-old question: "What if?" Pulled towards innovation, these makers maintain an unwavering devotion to a specific, often single material or form, but they choose to hack, exploit, or optimize them in individual and mesmerizing ways, underscored by the aesthetics that define the Millennial generation.

The collision between craft and the by-products of the post-digital world is on full display in this group, which generates a puzzling and radiant indistinction between human and machine. The Betatesters are unafraid to capitalize on the qualities of classic materials with hybrid processes in ratios only known to them. Although Jolie Ngo and Vincent Pocsik use conventional materials—terra-cotta or porcelain in Ngo's case, wood in Pocsik's—the processes of their mark-making are obscure to the untrained eye. Their work is defined by a unique blending of digital processes like CNC milling, 3D modeling and printing, and time-honored analog techniques. Beyond pressing a button and guiding the mouse, a machine depends on "the hand," the means and symbol of human intervention, for real innovation and artistry. Before the mid-2010s, this tendency in design was associated primarily with industry and mass production, not with one-off art or design

objects. However, the use of post-digital tools by artists and designers has steadily increased since, becoming more accessible and commonplace in recent years. The idiosyncratic work of the makers we have included here stands apart from the predictable aesthetic homogenization developing as tools like CAD or virtual reality sculpting become more popular.

For the Betatesters, technology does not replace the hand; it leverages it. When designing her vessels, Ngo prioritizes honesty by preserving the strata generated by the clay 3D printer and any glitches that have occurred during the printing. But it is just as vital for her to reconnect with the material in a tactile way, by adding clay "stickers" and hand-applying dollops of extravagant glaze. In Pocsik's anthropomorphic furniture, hand-drawn illustrations rendered in 3D animation software are sent to the CNC machine for rough modeling. He then returns to finish the work using traditional woodworking techniques. These types of collaborations also allow for an impressive yield of one-of-a-kind pieces. Work from Betatesters like Ngo, Pocsik, and others helps break down any remaining stigma suggesting that digital or industrial tools invalidate their craft.

While materiality is an anchoring preoccupation for those in this category, the tension between the analog and the digital prompts the inspection of not only process but also surface. The Betatesters convey varying levels of deception in their work, some through internet-adjacent aesthetics that belie the role of the hand. Mallory Weston produces pixelated palm fronds by hand-cutting anodized titanium pieces

Top: Jolie Ngo. *Flatpack Vessel in Wavy*, 2023. Stoneware and glaze (detail and full view on pp. 76–77)

Bottom: Vincent Pocsik. *Remember Your Hands*, 2022. Dyed black walnut and mirror (detail)

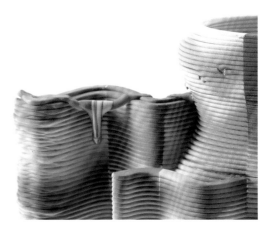

and hand-stitching them to leather. While they look straight out of a digital render, they are quite the opposite. The resulting flexibility is a material oxymoron, with hardness and softness coexisting; they are a wonder to handle. In reference to making, she calls herself a glutton: "I delight in laborious tasks; my obsessive techniques are an indulgence."[7]

Another sleight of hand lies in the material mimicry of Matthew Szösz's futuristic *Inflatables*. Fifteen years of experimentation have allowed the artist to engineer an untraditional technique of blowing glass with an air compressor that makes simple geometric shapes puff up into 3D forms that look like plastic. A still more overt disparity between what an object looks like and what it is made of—between inside and outside—is present in Joyce Lin's furniture practice, which is primarily concerned with the format of the chair. Her replication of one material using another (often epoxy clay made to look and feel like wood) verges on the compulsive. The resulting illusions trick the eye and surprise the hand, a benign riff on the fakery in much of our day-to-day media download.

Extraordinary transfiguration is an undeniable hallmark of this moment in contemporary art and design, a natural consequence of the changing definitions of tactility and our relationship to it. Without a doubt, "what we can engage with through 'touch' is rapidly evolving"[8] and, often, our first encounter with objects is through our screens. For better or worse, we have arrived at a state where we "metabolize" images so quickly—process, reprocess, and regurgitate them—that the procedure has become second nature, akin to staying hydrated. Because of the smartphone, we must be aware that "the traditional notions of art—its spatiality, its tactility, its dimensionality, its authenticity—are no longer the dominating attributes in how we look at visual work."[9] Instead, the odds are that images online, a democratic meta-version of objecthood, is how we find, share, and thus desire art, regardless of its real dimensions or materiality. The Betatesters challenge this state of affairs, doubling down on tactile sensory perception by creating objects with stimulating haptic qualities. Their flirtatious and, at times, duplicitous material compositions make their objects intriguing on the screen, but they are still better in person: looking begets the desire to touch.

Open-source vocabularies, defined by Millennial-age internet subcultures, flood the visual languages of many of

Left: Joyce Lin applying epoxy "bark" on a *Wood Chair*, 2023

Right: Matthew Szösz inflating a piece hot from the annealing oven at the WheatonArts Glass Studio during the *Emanation 2017* residency and exhibition project

the Betatesters, all of whom are digital natives. In some cases, cyberparadism, "an aesthetic that celebrates the power of human ingenuity and the beauty of the natural world,"[10] comes to mind. Pocsik, for example, uses the colors and scale of nature to generate links between people and our environment, while Weston's cyborg botanical jewelry investigates voyeuristic interactions on social media. This type of work encourages environmental consciousness, an optimistic relationship with technology, and a proclivity for augmentation. It all makes sense in a world where virtual and augmented reality are becoming ever more mainstream in gaming, education, and other sectors; more and more, we explore our natural surroundings from the comforts of our homes. Instead of exacerbating the argument around technology's persistent destruction of nature, this group provides another perspective: there is a strange paradox brewing as the digital and the "natural" converge. Together they make objects fit for hypernature, "an exaggerated simulation of a nature that never existed."[11]

The Betatesters look to define the "raw" materials of today and the future. This investigation is most evident in the practices of Brian Oakes, Layla Klinger, and Adam Grinovich. Oakes custom-builds circuit boards to piece together layered, interactive lighting fixtures, articulated by a mass of electrical cords. They aestheticize once complex but now commonplace and taken-for-granted technologies, of which they say, "There's never been a time before right now where me, as a single person, could get circuit boards made in a factory in Shenzhen that goes through the same standardization

as the circuit boards on in my phone."[12] Klinger, a fellow coder trained in lace making, upends that tradition by swapping thread for electroluminescent wire, making life-size doilies reactive to human touch. Finally, Grinovich translates his observations of fast-paced aesthetic shifts in sneaker culture—rubberized designs that suggest utility while being ornamental—onto engagement rings, one of the most recognized formats in jewelry.

Inherently enhanced, the Betatesters make 2.0 versions of "traditional" objects. They lean into the present moment, feeding our seeming urge to confuse and be confused, through dazzling sensory explorations that keep us guessing. Their collective inclinations also indicate a shift in norm about material sourcing within an ever-growing systems-oriented world and pose intriguing questions about the potential refuse of the future. What might we possibly make of it?

Top: The Cloud Forest is a conservatory and part of the Gardens by the Bay nature park in Singapore, built in 2012, which epitomizes the aesthetic and conceptual principles of cyberparadism

Bottom: Mallory Weston. *Shattered Begonia Brooch #1*, 2022. Anodized titanium, nickel, leather, and cotton

DOOMSDAYERS

In an election year, within a polarizing political environment, American apocalyptic anxiety is high. We have a new normal, in which politicians disseminate misleading or harmful rhetoric. Attacks on people of color, women, the LGBTQ+ community, and their rights are an everyday occurrence. Global warming is not a looming catastrophic event but an ever-growing reality, with parts of the world increasingly on fire or underwater. We live in dread of another pandemic, of artificial intelligence taking over, of book burnings and economic meltdowns. The list can go on and on. The Doomsdayers download these concerns into objects fit for a not-so-distant tomorrow, caught between dystopic angst and utopic optimism.

Like the Betatesters, the Doomsdayers use digital, industrial, and analog processes to make their work, which runs the gamut from ultra-sleek outer-space furnishings to ancient relics recontextualized for a future civilization. On one end of this spectrum, we have cartoonish hyper-objects designed by Ryan Decker that look as though they are still on-screen even when they sit right in front of us. At the opposite end, Cammie Staros's ceramic sculptures investigate how objects shape our understanding of humanity and past civilizations. Her "flooded" Greek amphoras foreshadow environmental reckoning, suggesting how the objects of today will become relics of the future.

The work of the Doomsdayers takes its meaning against the backdrop of a consumer landscape molded by capitalism, image oversaturation, and lightning-fast micro-trend cycles. It presents a query for object-makers: In a world where plastic waste negatively affects 88 percent of marine species[13] and over 146 million tons of garbage populate landfills worldwide,[14] why make more stuff? An August 2023 article on *Dazed Digital* put the current situation curtly: social media "trend cycles are attempting to remain on the cutting edge of uniqueness, while flattening all forms of individuality into a carefully selected collection of Amazon Storefront shoppable products that formulate a '-core' or 'girl' (sure to end up flooding Goodwill donation bins and landfills within a year)."[15] Phone-addicted Millennials and Gen-Zers are particularly trapped in this quandary.

For some Doomsdayers, making is a way to reconcile the illusion of choice, which capsizes our self-actualization and the chance for a sustainable future. Adam Grinovich's rubberized rings are made with parts that, in theory, are reusable or could even last forever, but ultimately pose the question of "which is worse?" as he swaps precious stones, historically

Installation view of Cammie Staros's exhibition *What Will Have Being* at Shulamit Nazarian, 2021

associated with conflict mining, for nonrecyclable and nondegradable materials to embellish the silver substructures (see p. 99). However, the material associations do more than just make a comment about eco-ethics or sustainability. Grinovich's work borrows from the exaggerated forms of the past decades' sneaker craze, and the enduring massive collaborations that have come with it, which shift their utility from a performance-driven object to one of luxury and status. He knows we have come to expect this consumerist cycle, and wants in. As his practice evolves, the jeweler hopes to similarly "liberate myself from the 'what's next' of it all,"[16] playing with the concept of infinite reiteration embedded in the pursuit of individuality.

The cybergrunge attitudes and aesthetics shared by the Doomsdayers show us how multiplicity acts both as a negative—as in irresponsible mass production, overconsumption, and overpopulation—and a positive, in terms of regeneration. By rejecting the conventional hierarchy of materials, Georgina Treviño turns the material surplus of our capitalist society and what many consider trash—an accumulation of cheap, mass-produced objects such as body-piercing jewelry, old CDs, and house keys—into post-Y2K treasures. Other times, she carves wax in the form of obsolete cult-like objects from the era, like flip phones, to cast in sterling silver, as if to make them immune to the destruction of time (see p. 108). Lilah Rose, in turn, renders abstracted piles of automobiles through quilted soft sculptures to critique prevailing conditions in Los Angeles, a city polluted and congested by car culture. She describes cars as "biological," like an overpopulated pest that she likens to the horror movie *The Cars That Ate Paris* (1974), where Frankensteined automobiles become monsters with faceless drivers in a plot to orchestrate car accidents in a hunt for scrap metal to sustain the local economy.[17] Images from the

Top: Vehicles departing the Burning Man festival in Black Rock City, Nevada, September 4, 2023

Left: Lilah Rose. *Corvetticus*, 2021. Satin, muslin, fabric dye, and poly-fil on canvas

disaster-struck Burning Man 2023 elucidate Rose's work outside a metropolitan context, where thousands of lined-up cars trying to leave Black Rock Desert were stuck in the mud for days. Can the thirty-seven-year-old event also be viewed as a potent microcosm for the neoliberal takeover of society at large? Speculations imply that what was once a free, leave-no-trace artistic paradise filled with costume, camaraderie, and community is now becoming more a gentrified, waste-generating playground for clout-chasers and the rich.

Many of the Doomsdayers reflect a twenty-first-century version of the popular sci-fi concept of a "used future," in which imaginative hyper-futuristic notions coexist with "dated" technologies from the present, as in the original *Star Wars* trilogy (1977–83), *Blade Runner* (1982), and *The Fifth Element* (1997). The works of Brian Oakes and Layla Klinger sharpen in such a context. Some of Oakes's cord-equipped and lighted sculptures move, record, and playback ambient noise. The abundance of electronics reminds us of global dependency, and of their potential as e-waste of the future. The transistors that give life to their work are microscopic; there are more of them "at work on this planet (some 15 quintillion, or 15,000,000,000,000,000,000) than there are leaves on all the trees in the world,"[18] an enormity that their work embraces. Klinger, who is also interested in salvaged and coded materials, has developed a process of "physical computing"[19] to produce people-scale, human-activated installations of augmented lace patterns. They construct maze-like spirals and enclosures using continuous lengths of filament to

mirror structures found in textiles, yet they remain unstable; the holes in the lace are defined by non-matter, which alludes to the potential for collapse. The concept of sequencing is twofold in their work. Technically, it determines the color-changing patterns of the sculptures, but it is also a nod to the history of the craft. Trained only in one or two bobbin sequences, the impoverished women who once made lace for the wealthy had to hand it off to someone else for it to be completed. Klinger's reference to this collaboration-as-subjugation has dystopian notes of both beauty and despair.

A video-game enthusiast, Decker primarily works digitally and virtually to design his wildly imaginative alien hybrids of industrial and internet landscapes outfitted with tentacles or plant-like appendages. More than surreal, the designer considers "landscapes as the original form of escapism."[20] An installation of his objects is like a life-size immersive multiplayer role-playing video game (see p. 117). Decker trolls the disintegrating human-made world around us by proposing an outlandish second option. His work recalls *isekai*, a subgenre of video games, manga, and anime (and phenomenon in literature) where

Left: Brian Oakes. *Vessel 1*, 2022. Printed circuit boards, electronic components, microphones, audio cables, custom 3D-printed hardware, power supplies, chain, and miscellaneous hardware

Right: Layla Klinger. *Infinite Pollination (Rose 02)*, 2022. Electroluminescent wire, wrapping wire, LDR sensors, and EL Sequencer (work in progress)

characters are suddenly sucked through a portal and plopped into another world or realm. The reverse can be said when viewing his individual objects isolated, outside the virtual fantasy land from which they came. "I want it to look like they've been transported from another location. . . . They reflect their [original] environment, so you're only looking at their subject matter."[21]

Despite the ominous name we have given them, our Doomsdayers are planners, prop-makers, and world-builders, designing hypothetical optimizations to our world through a post-digital lens. Few are pessimistic. On the contrary, Amia Yokoyama and Sulo Bee proactively take control of their own fates. Operating according to the video game premise of "respawning," where an avatar does not die but reappears in another location, Yokoyama's porcelain femmes have power in numbers. She rejects linear constructs of time and space, like Decker, preferring the fluid landscapes of manga, anime, and digital animation, where glitches function as points of origin for alternative realities. Her obsidian sculptures, which project green holographic images of her recurrent archetypes, are portals to a world of her own making. Similarly, Sulo Bee has invented a nirvanic realm called "$P4RKL3_FiLTH_CL0UD_NiN3," a domain free from binaries and populated by their jewelry. Their large-scale lightweight pendants, made using analog processes like electroforming and spray-painting, render detritus into cheerful queer hieroglyphs for the future (see p. 122).

Other Doomsdayers hint at the endless cycle of dissolution and creation through the attributes of their forms, which appear distorted, melting, shifting, or somehow in flux. These visual glitches manifest in the undulating form of Staros's vessels, the gooey surfaces and fleeting images of Yokoyama's sculptures, and the play between 2D and 3D in Decker's furniture. It can also be sensed in Chen Chen and Kai Williams's *Transition Mirrors*. The design duo sources uncut rocks and minerals that they slice, bond to glass, and then surround with pooled silver nitrate, with their edges seeming to evaporate. Gravity and chance individualize each piece, like the product of some kind of industrial, extraterrestrial material spill.

Myra Mimlitsch-Gray's tabletop pieces, like *Melting Candelabrum*, appear to be the result of extreme heat. But contrary to its molten appearance, the work is hollow and light. In fact, she

Left: Myra Mimlitsch-Gray. *Melting Candelabrum*, 2003. Silver. Rotasa Collection Trust

Right: Amia Yokoyama. *Tower (Accumulation)*, 2022–23. Porcelain, stoneware, and glaze (detail and full view on p. 120)

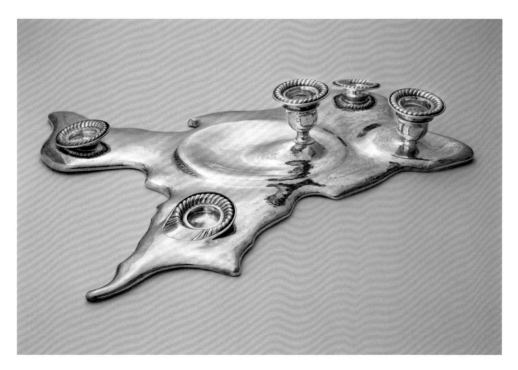

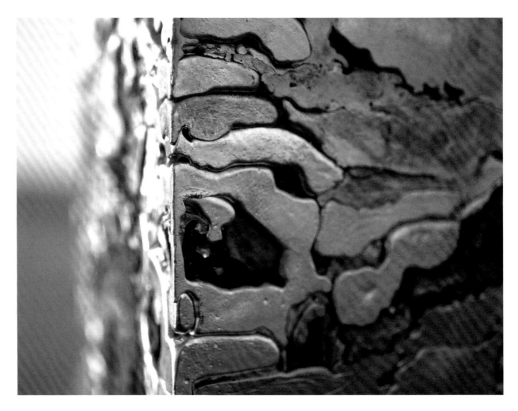

MJ Tyson. *93 Crestwood Road*, 2017. Personal objects left behind by the deceased residents of 93 Crestwood Road (detail)

solders and hand-raises all elements from a sheet of silver. This process induces a remarkable twisting of assumptions that sparks hope despite the debilitated external appearance of the object. But the idea of being "in flux" is perhaps best encapsulated in MJ Tyson's vessels and jewelry. Her melted-down metal objects extend the tradition of Victorian memento mori jewelry, reminding us of the transient nature of human life. The protruding prongs of a fork, the edge of a plate, the face of a coin: these apparitions in the layers of melted metal provide glimpses into the past lives of objects no longer valued. Tyson gives them a second life.

When the Burning Man "Mudpocalypse" hit the playa, outsiders were quick to assume the worst of those left behind: disorder, theft, resource guarding. That, however, did not come to be. History has proven that in the face of communal disaster, people "altruistically cooperate"[22] to help one another. Though the objects in this category might at first appear to reflect a grim reality, existential dread, or some kind of "no future," they can also be seen as a call for connection and IRL togetherness. For the Doomsdayers, chaos is not the end, but a portal to a new beginning.

INSIDERS

Outfitted with a lifetime of interacting with the domestic realm, object makers are especially primed to subvert our relationship with it. It escapes no one that this relationship has been tested to an extreme in recent history, given the prolonged imposed time indoors, often in isolation, during the COVID-19 lockdown. We are still recovering from this sudden shift, which increased loneliness and dependency on our screens for voyeuristic purposes. However, it also gave us a collective sense of introspection that prompts rejection of the aforementioned fate. The Insiders' objects bring us back to an embodied reality, where we animate the things around us as characters and companions. Their objects play tricks on the expectations of objecthood within domestic bliss—sometimes going as far as effecting social change from the intimate space of the home, a sort of stealth tactic. Together, they present a funhouse of daring meta-objects that urge us to think about our everyday domestic surroundings and how, in turn, they affect human interiority. The makers that define this category create a fantastical tableau vivant, in which objects are anything but passive.

We know that domestic spaces have long been the subject of creative expression. Women artists, in particular, have repeatedly intervened in response to the historical subservience of the domestic realm. Critical works like Judy Chicago's *Dinner Party* (1974–79) and Liza Lou's full-scale beaded *Kitchen* (1991–96) argue for the value of women's labor or "women's work," both in time-consuming craft disciplines like beading, embroidery, and porcelain painting, as well as cooking, cleaning,

and hosting. Many of the Insiders make similarly home-coded objects of protest. Myra Mimlitsch-Gray takes the formal traditions, implied roles, and social functions associated with tableware and throws them completely out the window. *Party Barge*, a silver serving tray with too many handles, is in a state of anarchy (see p. 139). It is the latest example in a decades-long oeuvre in sterling silver, cast iron, enameled metal, and other kitchenware-related materials. In Francesca DiMattio's maximalist ceramic sculptures, facsimiles of everyday objects—laundry detergent bottles, garbage bags, and the odd shoe—fuse with vessels and clay-extrusions-as-shag-carpet. She covers her topsy-turvy amalgamations in recognizable historical ceramic patterns of the European elite, such as Sèvres and Wedgwood, destabilizing hierarchies of value and relishing in decorative overload (see p. 142).

Insiders subvert household objects by aestheticizing their functionality. Lighting a candlestick atop one of Roxanne Jackson's stacked and towering holders would require a stepladder. Like DiMattio, she combines surprising elements, such as cakes, vessels, or a witch's garb, to dismantle expectations of ceramics as utilitarian, embracing horror and fantasy as valid forms of femininity. Do these accumulations mock our post-COVID life and its nocturnal shopping sprees, fueled by an arbitrary need to adorn our live/work environments? Or perhaps they echo niche decor trends from TikTok, where social-media users source food-themed objects (including croissant lamps, martini tables, and corncob stools) and giant versions of pencils and

toothbrushes, for no other reason than to delight in their absurdity. Katie Stout is very much aligned with this phenomenon, with her charmingly odd furniture and objects, including a lamp in the style of Giuseppe Arcimboldo's paintings. Tiny ceramic fruits and vegetables make up the body of a cartwheeling figure, with glass flowers sprouting from its feet and hiding the lightbulbs. While Stout's objects are home-minded, they are no wallflowers. Her off-kilter characters seem eager to make a mess and become the center of attention in any room they enter.

Perpetuated by memes, the algorithm, and doomscrolling, the growing DIY spirit of internet users is also worth mentioning, especially of those who share the thrill of a guest-bathroom makeover, or a thrift store flip of mid-century modern furniture. As this kind of independent media continues to blend the transfer of goods and services with concepts of infinitely consumable "entertainment," it is getting harder and more confusing to really know what one needs in order to define an authentic sense of place and self.

This is true for creators and consumers alike. Collin Leitch's 3D-printed plastic and mahogany "entertainment centers," purposely mixing and matching design vocabularies found in vintage TV housing, make an astute comment about this conundrum (see p. 155). What do the animations of scanned filmed negatives show us on the tilted, glitched-out screens? Leitch, who has a background in filmmaking, is fascinated by the intertwined history of the television as a piece of furniture, and video art as a television program. He says, "Early video art, which had much political context, would've been displayed on a wood panel television within an art gallery context. It's the same kind of TV set that would be in any American household, where people were getting news about the Vietnam War. It is just so loaded."[23] It is a surreal thought, especially against the backdrop of vapid device dependency and the isolation that tends to surround it.

Loneliness is a theme present in Anne Libby's work, with her focus narrowing on an exploration of another mundane household object: the window. Her sculptural blinds made of highly polished steel contort and extend, reflecting their surroundings instead of providing privacy, which creates an introspective environment that forces us to look inward (see p. 158). Interrogating our behavior, the work adds to the dialogue about gaze, perception, our growing collective obsession with the presentation of self, and our voyeuristic tendencies to bear witness to the banalities of others. The evidence lies in the endless live streams, makeup tutorials, "Get Ready with Me"[24] videos, and other monotonous content recorded inside the bathroom, the bedroom, or the kitchen for millions of strangers to watch through the comfort of their screens.

What we put inside our house signals how we want people to perceive us. As we see more of what others have, this naturally influences what it is we want. The uptick of accessibility to viewing homes and their interiors, especially of the nouveau riche, reveals that many are cookie-cutter McMansions or pseudo-Scandinavian, devoid of personal style. Carl D'Alvia's colorful forms play a tug of war between the minimal and the ornate to troll this lack of point of view. Some sculptures look ready to bounce off the walls, others slouch in exasperation, as a humorous rift on artwork considered the epitome of art collecting in Hypebeast culture— a modern version of conspicuous consumption where pop stars and rappers become tastemakers. Newer versions of his gestural sculptures, like *Trundle* (see p. 168)*,* have been finished with tufted upholstery to appear more like living room furniture. The piece seems to be curling up and stretching, reflecting D'Alvia's wonderment: "What if the couch had its own idea?"[25]

Linda Nguyen Lopez's chunky, mosaic-tiled benches with integral lamps invite you to sit a while. As within D'Alvia's practice, her work refutes the assumption that objects are inanimate. Instead, for her they are fellow inhabitants with whom we can cultivate meaningful relationships. This point of view reflects her upbringing as the daughter of a Vietnamese mother and a Mexican father, where the common household language was an "imaginatively fragmented"[26] English. "The things that surround you, make you who you are," she has said. "Trying to understand my identity has always been a part of that—trying to understand who I was in a very Americanized home."[27] As such, she made friends with the objects around the house. Her tiles are hand-cut in the shape of textile motifs from both sides of her heritage. It is a subtle nudge to a lifetime of putting together the pieces of herself. As objects have supported Lopez in shaping her story, her hard-to-ignore blobby lamps double as incognito furniture, offering a space for others to contemplate their own stories.

Then there is Hugh Hayden's work, which meditates on the realities of the "American Dream" and what it means to be a Black American, based on his personal story. His sculptures might take the shape of commonplace household objects, but he always incorporates an element of surprise. Wicker baskets connecting to Southern craft traditions become basketball hoops, which then turn into the peacock chair of Black Panther Party leader Huey P. Newton (see p. 175). Iron skillets have faces in reference to African masks to delineate the roots of Southern cuisine. Though the work is surrealist, it is not illogical; saturated with cultural references, the objects have agency.

"I've grown accustomed to thinking of domestic objects as things that can carry resonance or memory within them individually, as well as in relation to each other. Through [my training in] poetry, I became particularly interested in how spatial memory is constituted through the juxtaposition of remembered objects,"[28] says Liam Lee. His needle-felting practice creates objects that "produce an immediate, primal response"[29] that exude familiarity and yet

Installation view of Carl D'Alvia's exhibition *Fundamentals* at HESSE FLATOW, 2022

are uncanny. Lee's practice represents a marriage of indoor and outdoor, and natural and human-made, where he looks to animate the sculptural forms and tapestries through the alchemical principle of spontaneous generation (see p. 165). While they may look alien within a domestic context, the plush, vibrant, otherworldly wool chairs are more than suitable for human use.

The Insiders do not make inconspicuous objects. As noted about theater director Robert Wilson's stage furniture, design can operate "beyond mere props, not only as characters within the performance, but also as sculptural objects that invite interpretation and contemplation—especially outside of their original context."[30] The artists presented here turn objects we thought we knew all too well suddenly unfamiliar. Their elaborate interfaces and exaggerated forms unlock a simulation of hyper-domesticity, one that teases and makes user satisfaction a curious feat. They destabilize domestic ideals with concerted agility to investigate the human-to-object relationships we take for granted. With dissidence and wonder, the Insiders reveal the domestic environment as a surreal state, a stage on which their furnishings—and sculptures of furnishing—play to our dreams, our desires, and our insecurities.

The artists and designers in this category address a big question about our surrounding environment: Where do we stand in society? By creating objects that impact the space they inhabit and challenge how we interact with them, the Mediators force us to evaluate not only our spatial awareness but also our identities. In other words, objects are symbols of the things we do and that happen to us, the central masses orbited by our life experiences. The Mediators amplify scale to make us more conscious of our bodies, catalyzing consideration of how we navigate physical, interpersonal, and collective space. While they may conjure atmospheres of play, contemplation, or rest, they are also working double time as personal, cultural, or political reckonings to which we must bear witness.

Linda Nguyen Lopez's story illustrates the captivating hidden narratives that lie behind objects, including her own. Any object, author Italo Calvino once observed, can be a crucial narrative link "that establishes a logical relationship of cause and effect."[31] In this way, an inanimate thing can be "the real protagonist of the story. . . . Around the magic object, there forms a kind of force field that is in fact the territory of the story itself."[32] As Calvino suggests, we habitually imbue objects with experience-informed meaning. This is clear in many of the poetically disruptive pieces by Hugh Hayden. His picnic tables and dining sets come with protruding branches or thorns that prevent you from sitting or gathering (see pp. 176–77). Other times it is elementary school chairs that have been conjoined and severely skewed, as if caught in an interference field. They provoke a

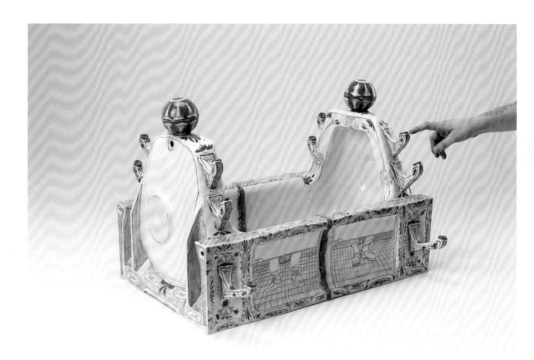

Nicki Green. *A Discrete History of Intimacy and Violence (double urinal basin with faucets)*, 2019. Glazed vitreous china and epoxy

visceral response but are also personal responses; the artist's feelings about disproportionate access to education and other socioeconomic disparities are palpable in his work. His pieces heighten bodily awareness, demanding us to consider what it means to be in the body that we have.

Nicki Green facilitates further self-examination. "I want people to have an experience of embodiment. Even though my experience is steeped in queerness, transness, Jewishness, I don't think those specifics need to be inhabited to engage with the work."[33] Her lavishly adorned earthenware tubs and composites of lavatory furnishings are reminders of the constant flux of physical matter, including our bodies, as well as personal transformation. She decorates her majolica-covered containers with lavender illustrations, a wink to the history of the color in the queer community, to make them as ornate as liturgical objects. The dressed-up containers become sacred spaces for transformation, drawing from the mikvah bathing ritual (traditionally for women) from her own Jewish culture.

Reclamation of space is central to Wally Dion. He turns stained-glass-like star quilts—symbols of honor in many Indigenous communities—into flags that, when installed, signal respect for the permeable prairie ecosystems that many Indigenous people depend on. Globally, the flag has played a charged role in colonialism, even during the Space Age. As a symbol, it proclaims allegiance, exudes power, and exerts ownership, often in places that it should not. Dion inverts colonial logic with his versions of flags that express loyalty to sacred nature and mark a reclamation of Indigenous land. Flown at Wanuskewin Heritage Park in 2022, *Grass Quilt*, the first in the series, became a billowing analogy of the intrinsic, nomadic potential of quilts, communally shared objects that "move, comfort, and most importantly, embrace the body. It signifies layers of story and experience that require activation and interaction."[34]

Like Dion, Jason McDonald and Norman Teague tackle ideas of space in relation to identity; they share a nexus of individual and community concerns around visibility and critical progress.

Wally Dion. *Grass Quilt*, 2022. Various fabrics

This pursuit isn't surprising; the number of prominent artists of color working in national and international design is embarrassingly small. Since 2020, the nonprofit, volunteer-run advocacy group WATBD? (Where are the Black Designers?) has been challenging this reality; their mission is "to heal, support, amplify, and make space for the entire spectrum of Black creativity while also decolonizing design through education and wellness resources, events, partnerships, and collaborations."[35] On the basis of data gathered from the 2021 AIGA design census, less than 5 percent of designers in the United States are Black.[36]

Glass artist McDonald addresses the boundaries imposed on micro (art world) and macro levels (society) due to systemic racism through sculptures, using the language of ironwork. Peppered with delicate, decorative canework elements, the baroque portals are beautiful but symbolize a barrier. His fragile gates ask: Are you the gatekeeper (inside) or the denied (outside)? The sculptures address the problematic gatekeeping that has stunted the growth of glassblowing in the Black community. Leaving the gate ajar, he welcomes other artists in (see p. 186). In November of 2022, Teague presented *Diasporic Mural*—a large wall piece made with African fabrics as part of his "Objects for Change" installation at the Art Center Highland Park, a community center that emphasizes "the importance of breaking down barriers"[37] (see p. 191). Like flags and monuments, a mural is another historically recognized large-scale expressive format that inspires communal moments of pause, reflection, and enjoyment. This dynamic is also built into his furniture-scaled objects. The *Sinmi* stools and *Africana* chairs are rockers that spark engagement, inviting the user to assume an unconventional yet restful posture *(sinmi* literally means to "relax" in the Yoruba language). Teague knows that such swaying motions have proven beneficial to our senses—think of rocking a baby to sleep, or a child oscillating on the swings at the playground. Often opting for more permeable, education-oriented spaces for his projects, he shows us that context matters. His objects invite agency, joy, and togetherness, a purposeful strategy to evoke social change and empowerment.

Justin Favela finds similar potential in the piñata, a popular symbol of celebration. His festive tapestries and immersive installations celebrate his Latine heritage while spoofing the art-historical canon that has historically prioritized white artists. His to-scale levitating fringed lowriders that gesture to the showmanship of the tricked-out cars are impossible to ignore. They are a bold statement that recontextualizes Chicano culture as a valuable element of American culture, especially in light of discriminatory codes that made lowriders illegal in California from 1958 to 2023.

If we look at objects as opportunities for rest, joy, and change, we must also look at where that offer is coming from: Does the meaning of those objects change depending on who made them? It is essential to consider the context of social or cultural community discussions. Some objects are as privileged as their makers; they simply get to exist, without making a statement for an entire social or cultural group. Our Mediators thus stage an argument against what Bayo Akomolafe describes as "white stability," a state where the vast majority has been convinced that "we are isolated independent selves" such that we no longer can see that "our bodies are coterminous with each other. . . . It flattens the world to make it convenient for isolated bodies to walk, and then it tells us that we're all alone."[38]

It is reflecting on notions such as Akomolafe's and of proxemics—the study of the nature and effect of the spatial separation between individuals and of how this separation relates to environmental and cultural factors—that Luam Melake makes her graphic, colorful furniture. Her *Love Seat in Two Parts*, as its title implies, has two modular components that can mirror the state of a relationship: together or apart (see p. 204). She shares that "there are studies that say if you're sitting three feet away from someone, you might interact differently than if you are five or six feet away."[39] Through the play with space and the interaction of bodies

Justin Favela. *Gypsy Rose Piñata*, 2017. Found objects, cardboard, Styrofoam, paper, and glue

Dee Clements installing a private commission at 167 Green Street in Chicago, 2023

with the modular components of her furnishings, Melake looks to unlock something unknown about our relationship to intimacy, and the distance that we put between ourselves and others, which is particularly poignant after the lockdown and isolation of the COVID-19 pandemic.

Although most of the Mediators address social issues at large informed by their identities, it is important that people not assume that an artist with a politicized body must be making work about an overtly political issue. As Melake, Dee Clements is speaking instead to something broader, in her case through a practice ingrained with the social history of women. As an avid researcher of craft through a feminist lens, she became more and more fascinated with basketry, especially its classification as "women's work." Clements started by making tighter forms closer to the source but has loosened up over the years and expanded her scale to let basketry run wild. The sculptures are "bulbous or oblong, droopy, saggy, leaning, bent, have folds, rolls, and

lumps"[40] to reference women's bodies and their experiences, especially the thankless chores they perform. Her expressive and voluptuous 3D forms made of hand-dyed reeds remain respectful to the history of women's labor and innovation while making space for women to have the freedom to do whatever they want.

A desire to challenge the perception of body, mind, and heart unifies the Mediators. Whatever the driving force, their objects ask: Will you walk around it, through it, or turn your back . . . or do you dare face what is before you? Some make the confrontation easier than others. Like with Melake, aspects of modularity—the concept of breaking down complex systems into smaller parts—is one way artists give us access to what lies behind their work, one piece at a time. And as we will see next, this can also happen through the creation of personal symbols and coded languages awaiting interpretation. Once you start looking, you might just find them everywhere.

CODEBREAKERS

Many objects are made complex through masked systems of communication. The Codebreakers solve puzzles but also make them, piecing together their own feelings or identities and leaving clues for others to figure out. For many, the analogy is anchored by construction methods decipherable to the eye. The repetition of these elements becomes the primary components that make a composition whole. For others, the meaning of their work is intentionally veiled by the final form an object takes, or through embedded personal symbology. Their readability can vary from transparent to opaque, like a code with varying levels of difficulty to crack. Echoing the human urge to organize, and thus better understand the world around us, the Codebreakers take a "more than the sum of its parts" approach to the extreme by building sorted but complex works, each with its own passcode.

Designer and artist Misha Kahn is a professional shapeshifter, oscillating with ease between mediums, materials, formats, scale, and applications. His practice is adaptive, running the gamut between furniture, sculpture, public artworks, jewelry, installations, and more, all of which are made from everything but the kitchen sink. The common denominator of his practice makes Kahn a Codebreaker: the compulsion to tinker and create his personal version of order where there is chaos. His approach is modular, as artworks or furniture pieces are the products of smaller, at times independently designed subsystems that work together as one. This happens both literally and figuratively in *Penny Dish,* a large ceramic-tiled object born

as a hypothetical computer-generated response to bureaucratic systems allegedly formed to serve us. It is a made-up problem with a made-up solution (note the teeny-tiny drawer for "lost change"). In fact, many of his works opt to satisfy what the artist calls our "primal need to drop something inside of something else,"[41] fill holes, find that perfect fit, whatever it may be.

Putting things away is a relative and arbitrary inclination for us all. Whether you are a "filer or piler," the small feeling of accomplishment and other mental rewards that come with being tidy help combat our ever-fractioning focus that a life attached to a computer screen has subjugated us to. Organizational systems that are efficient to one person might appear nonsensical to another, but they are united by our universal urge to place, stack, and sort. Ranging from playful to methodical, sometimes compulsive, the Codebreakers present their interpretations of this phenomenon.

Misha Kahn. *Penny Dish*, 2022. Ceramic

Opposite: Richard Chavez. *Cuff*, 2000. Black jade, coral, turquoise, and sterling silver

Glass artist Cedric Mitchell and woodworker Trey Jones, like Kahn, make work akin to futzing with building blocks, tinker toys, or jigsaw puzzles, in sophisticated ways. Mitchell blows color-saturated symmetrical forms one by one, and only after amassing a selection does he decide which elements belong with which, and their order. He then fuses them together to create neatly stacked tabletop pieces, whose post-Memphis associations only strengthen their modular compositional quality. The mix and match of the shapes reflects the glassblower's propensity for remixing diverging inspirations from funk music to 1990s toy aesthetics (see p. 211). Jones, on the other hand, works with scrap plywood, which he stacks together over and again to make furniture. It is his version of Japanese *nerikomi*, the practice of slicing through pigmented layers of clay to reveal patterning. After the cutting, like a woodworker's version of mesmerizing binary code, dazzling geometries appear and add depth to his pieces, which are also interactive (see p. 215). Using upcycled materials also solves a personal problem for the designer, who says, "While contemplating my practice, I jokingly imagined that the definition of hell was being forced to live the same life over again but with only everything you cast away in your past life. I saw a lot of scrap plywood in my personal hell—and felt empowered to change that."[42]

In practices such as these, patience and a painstaking but worthwhile process are appreciated. This is something Richard Chavez knows all about, an architect turned jeweler who specializes in lapidary work. Though Chavez is from San Felipe Pueblo, he was taken by jewelry made in the Navajo style. Characterized by compositions of perfectly cut, fit, and polished minerals set in silver or gold, the jeweler was determined to teach himself the precisions of the trade. Decades later he is a leading hand in his chosen craft. His pared-down, impeccably seamless bracelet

in black jade, turquoise, and coral has a modern edge that triumphs within what he calls the "dominant society," or outside of a specifically Indigenous context of which he is proud of.[43] (It is important to note, however, that Native American artists and craftspeople have developed thriving spaces to share and market their work, apart from, but at times overlapping, mainstream centers of art.) Like decluttering, Chavez succeeds in reducing his forms down to their essence. They are no more than they need to be.

Kim Mupangilaï and Steven KP also work in simplified ways to change people's relationships with their identities. Mupangilaï's practice presents a synthesis of her heritage, which she retrofits together through the assemblage of four specific materials; the designer, who grew up in Europe with a Belgian mother and Congolese father, makes furniture in teak, stone, rattan, and banana fiber (see p. 224). The materials are symbols of the Democratic Republic of Congo, where they are commonly used in domestic applications. These choices are efforts to reconcile her upbringing disconnected from half of her heritage, and as woman of color in a predominantly white country—not to mention the sordid history between her parents' homelands. The artful interlocking of meaningful materials conveys the process of reconnecting with her roots while resisting assimilation into Western culture. But her smooth, surreal, anthropomorphic forms, seemingly conscious and empathetic, make sense there too. They are code-switchers—adaptive objects that make sense to certain people at certain times for certain reasons, "hop-scotching between different cultural and linguistic spaces and different parts of our own identities."[44]

Sometimes the meaning of objects is only there for those who can see it. Working reductively, KP's jewelry—knots and strings made from wood—explores mechanisms for passing and signaling, concepts heavily ingrained in queer

culture. What we wear can send a message of solidarity, or in turn single us out to different people. With coded objects in mind, KP's knots are reminiscent of Oscar Wilde's green carnation. Although now famously remembered as a symbol of gay fashion, its mysterious and secret meaning was unbeknownst to many even at the height of its popularity. Whittling the forms is also how the artist works through past trauma, and the *Partially Undone* series symbolizes that journey. At first glance it may not be evident that KP's unraveling knots are frozen at a certain point within that action. They hand-carve blocks of solid wood, in a process that allows them to "embrace the tenderness and slowness that working with it required."[45] The symbolic nature of their work is trifold, as KP maintains the woodcarving tradition that their grandfather taught them.

Jordan Nassar's practice is a persistent effort to remain connected to his Palestinian heritage from a diasporic perspective. His meticulously embroidered wall panels depict distant mountains and sunsets of all colors. The cross-stitching of recurrent decorative motifs and patterns creates fragmentary views, as if looking through a mesh screen depicting utopian visions of his ancestral homeland. To create these works, Nassar uses Palestinian needlework techniques of the *tatreez*, and collaborates with women in the West Bank to embroider the traditional borders on his canvases (see p. 231). He carries forth a cultural heritage while subverting expectations of a matrilineal craft. Through the calm and repetitive process, manifestation is made physical

Steven KP. *Partially Undone Knot*, 2020. Ebonized American cherry wood, deerskin leather, and 14-karat gold

as though he is writing his own code to generate the future he desires. His more recent endeavors in wood inlay using brass and mother-of-pearl are an equally precise and deliberate process that adds a more stable element to the temporality of his vision.

It is through the making of encrypted objects that the Codebreakers establish agency over their own "script," increasing their sense of autonomy and defining what is worth carrying into the future. Through their complex practices, they can process who they are, how they see the world, and how they want the world to see them back. It is a temporal journey where the act of putting things together, piece by piece or stitch by stich, may deliver a solution, a resolution, or even a comprehensive reimagining.

The Keepers have stories to tell and objects to do the storytelling. These artists and designers recognize that intangible entities such as identity, memory, and connection are at risk of dissipating without proper care and documentation. The objects in this category embody these concepts, and their creation makes them tangible. Concerned with preserving cultural and personal stories, whether heritage, vernaculars, or traditional craft practices, through unexpected formats, the makers in this group have developed methods of transferring knowledge at risk of being lost to time. The Keepers are time-travelers fusing past and present into artifacts for the future.

Coulter Fussell's quilting practice began from a desire to make something for her children, as her mother and her mother before her had done. Without the resources to buy materials, she put out a call for donations. Locals began dropping off their clothes and linens for Fussell to transform into experimental quilts. The work has become more outlandish with time as the objects arriving at her studio become more dimensional and diverse. Photographs, old mail, frames, and skateboards are just some of the items she incorporates, saying, "They're all on an even playing field simply because they've shown up to my door at my studio."[46] She jigsaws these objects together to make quilts that tell her own stories of motherhood and growing up in the South (see p. 234). Her practice preserves not only objects but also the stories entrenched in them. Her neighbors trust that their donations will avoid the landfill, instead becoming communal heirlooms about Southern life and women's labor.

Joyce J. Scott. *Voices*, 1993. Glass beads, thread, chain, and synthetic faceted discs. The Museum of Arts and Design, New York; purchase with funds provided by the Horace W. Goldsmith Foundation, 1994.48

Celebrated artist Joyce J. Scott is also a visual storyteller, whose jewelry and glass sculptures crystallize critical perspectives about race in the US. Best known for her statement neckpieces, she brings narratives to life through the peyote stitch—a beading technique used by Native American communities, with the earliest examples dating to Egyptian times. Her subversive figurative stories confront American racial stereotypes. While Fussell argues for commemorating not just the big moments but the small intimate ones with inconspicuous objects, Scott demonstrates that even the ugly side of the truth is worth remembering.

For Pauline Shaw, remembrance is fickle. Her practice investigates memory and personal histories as a first-generation Asian American through a spiritual and scientific lens. Her large-scale, sometimes monumental, felted tapestries are attempts to reconstruct fragmented memories supplemented by images from MRI scans—a visual, albeit abstract, record of where humans store memories. Her dense panels go in and out of focus as if depicting the corruption of memory, acknowledging that we are unreliable narrators, even of our own lives (see p. 242). However fuzzy the memories may be, she gives them permanence through materiality. The psychedelic patterning of her feltings comes from craft-based practices such as historical textiles, Chinese paper cutting, lacemaking, and marbling, which she combines with glass elements.

The Keepers diffuse back to where we started by working in ancient disciplines with material honesty. They carry on traditional or historical languages but with a marked twist. Vernaculars are often remixed with unexpected iconography, translated into a different material or undergoing purposeful distortion. From far away, one of Roberto Lugo's large-scale pieces might fool you as a Greek black-and-red-figure vessel. Upon closer inspection, however, the scenes unfolding in the round are not epic battles, but an architectural rendering of his neighborhood in Philadelphia. With the *Orange and Black* series, Lugo addresses how systemic racism informs the American judicial system, with the color palette representing a riff on prison uniforms. Renowned for interpolating the visual language of historical styles of ceramics with graffiti and images of famous Black and Brown politicians, athletes, or hip-hop artists, he stages a dialogue about value and desire in American society. Lugo's pottery is commemorative not only of the figureheads in the public eye but of the communities they represent. In that way, his work is a love poem to where he grew up; Lugo's bequest lies in making ceramics more relevant to his community.

The works in this category are not about replication, but about making an object that will carry on a legacy—and not an ego-driven one but one about community, lineage, and heritage. The

Roberto Lugo. *The Day I Tried to Play Baseball*, from the *Orange and Black* series, 2023. Glazed stoneware

makers are intentional about what they preserve, which is typically tied to their personal histories and identities. For example, Anina Major's practice at its core intertwines with who she is and where she is from. Her serene braided, or "plaited," as she would say, ceramic vessels and sculptures bring basketry to mind (see p. 251). Away from her Bahamian motherland, Major looked to connect across water, time, and space. She developed a contemporary take on the decades-long straw-weaving tradition her grandmother practiced (as many other women did) at the tourist market to provide for her family, which originated with enslaved ancestors. Conscious that the natural materials degrade, Major's more durable alternative, clay, extends the life of a dying tradition where many regional vernaculars have gone out of style due to changing attitudes, demand, and the introduction of imported goods in the tourist market. Without context, Major's work is a beautiful vehicle for experimentation with different kinds of weaves and glazes reminiscent of the ocean, but with it, the pieces are a sure testament to her cultural inheritance. She says, "My work is charged with expanding our understanding of Afro-Caribbean Black identity and culture."[47]

Top: James Johnson. *Lákt (Transforming Raven)*, 2022. Yellow cedar and red cedar

Bottom: Students from Venancio Aragon's Intro to Navajo Weaving class at Diné College showcasing their work alongside the artist, 2023

In a similar way, Nicole McLaughlin is looking to defy expectations for women through fiber and ceramic. The plates in her sculptures have no other utility than to be vehicles for fiber with a nod to her personal and cultural history (see p. 254). Through the symbolism of the vessel that is often applied to women, her work carries forth craft traditions from her Mexican heritage. The flowing fiber connecting the plates symbolizes the transmission of knowledge and her matrilineal lineage, an act of "cultivation and preservation of what I think is important to my own identity."[48]

The descendant of a long line of Tlingit chiefs, James Johnson's wood-carving practice is a gesture to honor his ancestors. His masks, bentwood boxes, paddles, and panels are unmistakably Tlingit with carved animal iconography and abalone inlay, as well as painted in iconic shades of red, black, and teal. The work remains true to tradition in most senses. However, an aficionado of extreme sports, he applies this lexicon to a new format: snowboards and skateboard decks. It feels like a natural transition to decorate these young objects in the way of revered ancient technologies, such as canoes, which remain essential in

his culture. Through his work, Johnson spreads awareness of contemporary Indigeneity and Tlingit art.

For Venancio Aragon, his heritage is also a driving force, as he learned how to weave at a young age from his mother. Trained in the art of Navajo weaving, he uses the upright tension loom, another ancient Indigenous technology, to bring his technicolor tapestries to life. His rainbow palette and unrestrained approach produce saturated compositions for the social-media age. Aragon's graphic weavings serve as a "living record"[49] of his personal and cultural legacy of weaving. He is also invigorated by transferring this knowledge by teaching at Diné College. Venancio says it is a "tremendous gift for our people to relearn and revive parts of our culture. I learned that as an instructor of our cultural arts, every student is vital to the preservation and continuation of our people, and I am filled with hope for the next generation."[50]

We are in a moment in history where what we commemorate is under scrutiny and reformation, from the lasting presence of Confederate monuments and protests for their removal, to critiques over new sculptures. Of note

Robert E. Lee statue in Richmond, VA, during Black Lives Matter protests in 2020, with a projection of Harriet Tubman

are Hank Willis Thomas's *The Embrace* in Boston, recognizing the unity between civil rights leaders Martin Luther King Jr. and Coretta King, which received mixed reviews, and the open call for proposals for a new Harriet Tubman sculpture in Philadelphia after the original choice of a white artist sparked much debate. The Keepers' work proposes alternative models of acknowledging the importance of cultures, languages, and moments that are often dismissed or forgotten. They take it upon themselves to represent their histories, communities, and cultures by crafting future artifacts. They are living, growing, moving records that demonstrate how people and their legacies can live on through making objects. The objects are also reminders that their longevity depends on us: if not cared for properly with the inherited knowledge and tools to do so, they remain as ephemeral as our distant memories.

It is in this spirit that the catalog and exhibition for *Objects: USA 2024* make up a daring entry into the evolving chronicles of the history of art, craft, and design objects made in the US. The seven categories dissected in this essay represent new archetypes for contemporary approaches to making, which are bound to remain relevant well into the future. Their potential lies in their extended applications in better understanding creative practices outside of the stellar examples of this cohort. When brought together, the artists and designers celebrated here make objects that reveal an infinite feedback loop of the psyche of our current moment, and the hands that cannot remain idle.

NOTES

1 This was limited to artists of Asian, African American, Native American, and Latine heritage. About 55 percent of the small total number were Asian artists, with fewer Native and Black artists (about 17 percent each), and even fewer Latine artists (about 11 percent).

2 Ian Collings, interview by Kellie Riggs, October 21, 2023.

3 Hannah Martin, "Meet the Young Korean Designer Putting an Inventive Spin on Tradition," *Architectural Digest*, May 26, 2021, https://www. architecturaldigest.com/story/meet-the-young -korean-designer-putting-an-inventive-spin-on -tradition.

4 Lonnie Vigil, in SAR School for Advanced Research, "Grounded in Clay: Lonnie Vigil Conversation Part I," YouTube, August 23, 2022, https://www.youtube.com/watch?v=I8FiN1rIWvE.

5 Lonnie Vigil, in SAR School for Advanced Research, "Grounded in Clay: Lonnie Vigil Conversation Part II," YouTube, August 23, 2022, https://www.youtube.com /watch?v=NmfXpaaHs5E.

6 Jamie Bennett, interview by Kellie Riggs, September 30, 2023.

7 Mallory Weston, interview by Kellie Riggs, September 17, 2019.

8 Omar Kholeif, *Goodbye, World! Looking at Art in the Digital Age* (Berlin: Sternberg Press, 2018), 134.

9 Kholeif, *Goodbye, World!*, 173–74.

10 "Cyberparadism," Aesthetics Wiki, accessed October 24, 2023, https://aesthetics.fandom.com /wiki/Cyberparadism.

11 "Hypernature," Next Nature, accessed October 24, 2023, https://nextnature.net /magazine/themes/hypernature.

12 Brian Oakes, interview by Kellie Riggs, July 3, 2023.

13 Mine B. Tekman et al., *Impacts of Plastic Pollution in the Ocean on Marine Species, Biodiversity and Ecosystems* (Berlin: WWF, 2022), 9. http://dx.doi.org/10.5281/zenodo.5898684.

14 "Facts and Figures about Materials, Waste and Recycling," United States Environmental Protection Agency, December 3, 2022, https:// www.epa.gov/facts-and-figures-about-materials -waste-and-recycling/guide-facts-and-figures -report-about.

15 Caitlyn Clark, "Blueberry milk nails and the illusion of choice under capitalism," *Dazed Digital*, August 25, 2023, https://www.dazeddigital.com /beauty/article/60644/1/blueberry-milk-nails -illusion-of-choice-under-capitalism.

16 Adam Grinovich, interview by Kellie Riggs, October 3, 2023.

17 Lilah Rose, interview by Angelik Vizcarrondo-Laboy, March 10, 2023.

18 Simon Winchester, *Exactly: How Precision Engineers Created the Modern World* (Glasgow, UK: Harper Collins, 2019), 280.

19 Layla Klinger, interview by Kellie Riggs, October 4, 2023.

20 Ryan Decker, interview by Kellie Riggs, July 11, 2023.

21 Decker, interview.

22 Zeynep Tufekci, "One Thing Not to Fear at Burning Man," *New York Times*, September 3, 2023, https://www.nytimes.com/2023/09/03 /opinion/columnists/burning-man-rain-mud.html.

23 Collin Leitch, interview by Kellie Riggs, July 17, 2023.

24 As of January 2023, #GRWM (the hashtag and acronym for "Get Ready with Me") had more than 59.5 billion views on TikTok. Christian Allaire, "TikTok's 'Get Ready with Me' Videos Are a Comforting Phenomenon," *Vogue*, January 4, 2023, https://www.vogue.com/article/tiktok-get -ready-with-me-videos.

25 Carl D'Alvia, interview by Kellie Riggs, October 5, 2023.

26 "Linda Lopez," State of the Art: Discovering American Art Now, Crystal Bridges Museum of American Art, accessed October 30, 2023, https:// stateoftheart.crystalbridges.org/blog/project /linda-lopez/.

27 Ivy Vuong, "Leaving with Empathy: A Q&A and Studio Visit with Linda Lopez," *Blog*, Crystal Bridges Museum of American Art, August 19, 2022, https://crystalbridges.org/blog/leaving-with -empathy-a-qa-and-studio-visit-with-linda-lopez.

28 Liam Lee, "Questionnaire - Ogunquit Museum—Spontaneous Generation" (unpublished manuscript, Spring 2023), 1.

29 Lee, "Questionnaire," 1.

30 Ralph McGinnis, "For Theater Pioneer Robert Wilson, Chairs Are Characters. See Decades' Worth of His Stage Furniture at a Brooklyn Gallery," *Artnet News*, November 18, 2022, https://news.artnet.com/art-world/robert-wilson -theater-stage-chairs-2213158.

31 Italo Calvino, *Six Memos for the Next Millennium* (Boston: Mariner Books, 2016), 32.

32 Calvino, *Six Memos*, 32.

33 Nicki Green, interview by Angelik Vizcarrondo-Laboy, February 6, 2023.

34 "Wally Dion," Bonavista Biennale, accessed October 30, 2023, https://bonavistabiennale.com /artists/wally-dion/.

35 "About Us," WATBD?, accessed October 24, 2023, https://www.watbd.org/about-us.

36 "AIGA Design POV Learnings," AIGA, the professional association for design, accessed October 30, 2023, https://www.aiga.org/aiga -design-pov-by-the-numbers.

37 Vasia Rigou, "Spotlight in Design: Object Oriented at The Art Center Highland Park," *Newcity Design*, November 23, 2022, https:// design.newcity.com/2022/11/23/spotlight-in -design-at-the-art-center-highland-park/.

38 Bayo Akomolafe, in AGLN (Aspen Global Leadership Network) (@aspenagln) and ten (The Emergence Network) (@the_emergence_network), "On White Stability," Instagram video, August 22, 2023, https://www.instagram.com/p /CwQMJGzo3Pw/.

39 Hannah Martin, "Luam Melake's Foam Furniture Wants to Bring People Back Together," *Architectural Digest*, January 23, 2023, https:// www.architecturaldigest.com/story/luam -melakes-foam-furniture-wants-to-bring-people -back-together.

40 Dee Clements, "Biography," Nina Johnson Gallery, accessed October 30, 2023, https:// ninajohnson.com/artists/dee-clements/.

41 Misha Kahn, interview by Kellie Riggs, October 3, 2023.

42 "About," Trey Jones Studio, accessed October 30, 2023, http://treyjonesstudio.com/about.

43 Kari Chalker, *Totems to Turquoise: Native North American Jewelry Arts of the Northwest and Southwest* (Abrams: New York, 2004), 202.

44 Gene Demby, "How Code-Switching Explains The World," *Code Switch*, NPR, April 8, 2013, https://www.npr.org/sections /codeswitch/2013/04/08/176064688/how-code -switching-explains-the-world.

45 Steven KP, "So Mint! Bundles and Blanks and Binds and Bends by Steven KP," *Current Obsession*, August 24, 2020, https://www.current -obsession.com/so-mint-bundles-and-blanks -and-binds-and-bends-by-steven-kp/.

46 Coulter Fussell, interview by Angelik Vizcarrondo-Laboy, June 13, 2023.

47 Anina Major, interview by Angelik Vizcarrondo-Laboy, March 12, 2023.

48 Nicole McLaughlin, interview by Kellie Riggs, October 4, 2023.

49 Venancio Aragon, "Artist Statement," Venancio Aragon, October 10, 2023, https://www. venancioaragon.com/artist-statement.html.

50 Venancio Aragon (@aragontextiles), Instagram, October 8, 2023, https://www.instagram.com /aragontextiles/p/CyKePrTth8G/?img_index=1.

TRUTHSAYERS   TRICKSTERS   DOOMSDAYERS

Nik Gelormino

B. 1986, San Francisco, CA
Lives and works in Los Angeles, CA
nikgelormino.com
@nik_gelormino

Nik Gelormino's one-of-a-kind wooden objects possess a rare quality in art and design: sincerity. He transforms logs into playful furniture with a few simple gestures, bringing flowers, shells, and car shapes to life. However, his material choice is as important as the form. Gelormino sources naturally felled trees in Los Angeles to carve by hand, using chisels, knives, and hand planes. He primarily utilizes uncommon woods in furniture-making, such as eucalyptus and live oak.

Through skillful carving and polishing, he renders the hardy material smooth as butter in a signature puffy style. Every rhythmic mark from his tools is recorded on the caramel surfaces of his sculptural stools, drawing attention to the waving patterns inherent to the wood grain. He accentuates and sutures the natural cracks of the material with dovetail joinery made of contrasting wood species. The detail adds a whimsical touch, like resting butterflies on a tree stump, while remaining a genuine expression of the discipline of woodworking. Like Wharton Esherick and J.B. Blunk, famous woodworkers before him whom he admires, Gelormino is looking to connect humanity to nature in his practice.

—ANGELIK VIZCARRONDO-LABOY

Flat Car (no. 02), 2023. Fir

Opposite: *Shell Stool (no. 11)*, 2023. Ash

Top: Tools in Nik Gelormino's studio, 2024

Right: *Flower Stool (no. 03)*, 2021. Ash; *Shell stool (no. 04)*, 2021. Cedar

Opposite: Gelormino carving *Flat Dove (no. 02)*, 2024. Redwood

Ian Collings

B. 1985, Virginia Beach, VA
Lives and works in Ojai, CA
iancollings.com
@ian_collings

According to Ian Collings, rocks hold the highest level of consciousness because they've been watching it all. As a material that Collings works with his hands, slowly and responsively, stone has so much to give; it is the most durational, physical embodiment of time, outlasting the oldest living things. Locked deep inside its matter are millennia of geological and human history. Collings treats his samplings as though they've had their own lives. He yields to their individual volitions, their physical constitutions often domineering the artistic intention. The results are "not always pretty—which feels more honest. The stone is the teacher."[1]

Collings's general inclination is to accentuate the stone's inherent patterning by uncovering unique forms within, as in works like *Refigured Berry Bowl*. Other times, the results of his mark-making appear to quiver in motion. At first, that may feel like a delightful contradiction to the material's inherently still nature; rather, the effect can be experienced as sustained reverberations echoing the movement of time. Embracing this physicality has become a bigger and more important aspect of his practice, which more recently includes working less with rock merchants and going into the desert to cultivate the specimens himself instead. It is a constant dialogue, more of a paced collaboration than an intervention. It is in this way that Collings tries to escape the dislocation he feels within the acceleration of the human-built, human-centric world.

—KELLIE RIGGS

1 Ian Collings, interview by Kellie Riggs, October 21, 2023.

Movements - Stone Objects 06, 2023. Travertine

Opposite: *Refigured Berry Bowl*, 2022. Red marble

Top: Ian Collings working in his studio, 2020

Right: Installation view of *Movements* at The Future Perfect, San Francisco, 2023

Opposite, top: Works in progress in his studio, 2021

Bottom: *Movements - Untitled 01*, 2023. Red travertine

Minjae Kim

B. 1989, Seoul, Korea
Lives and works in Brooklyn, NY
minjae.kim
@mnjaekim

Minjae Kim's relationship to material has always been about what's accessible to him in the moment. Since the beginning of his sustained foray into furniture design, which picked up speed during the pandemic lockdown, the former architect and interior designer insists that wood is still the most plausible medium with which to work. In a world where people tend to quickly conflate meaning and intention, it's a sincere and unfussy statement of approach. The format of the humble chair, to which Kim has consistently stayed devoted, exhibits a similar sense of dependability. For him, chairs are an "immediately relatable"[1] object. In his renditions, even when the seat has been hand-carved in unexpected angles, viewers and sitters connect with them with ease. Kim is able to accentuate wood's inherent duality as a precision-based yet entirely free sculptural material with a playful and intuitive touch.

Making is also a grounding and connecting force for Kim, who grew up primarily in Korea and has expressed liminal feelings about his heritage and his life in America. This plays out more visually through his larger works in fiberglass, which he ingeniously quilts to create transparent lampshades and sconces that loosely resemble ceremonial Korean garb through a romanticized lens.

—KR

---

1 Minjae Kim, interview by Kellie Rigs, November 15, 2023.

Hull Table, 2023. Douglas fir, sapele, oak, and acrylic paint

Opposite: *Wrong Chair II*, 2023. Wood

Opposite: Chairs in the studio, 2023

Garb 4, 2023. Quilted fiberglass, resin, wood, pearl, brass, and lighting elements

Lonnie Vigil

B. 1949, Nambé Pueblo, NM
Lives and works in Nambé Pueblo, NM

Lonnie Vigil prefers rolling his coils in his hands rather than on the table. He likes it when his *puki* bowls and baskets leave their marks on the bottom of his pots. The lips of his vessels, in shimmering brown or black, break symmetry, slope, or flare. Finding his own language in the traditions of Pueblo pottery, his vessels are distinctly his own, and have transformed their role from merely utilitarian objects to highly collected prized works of art.

Vigil is a potter who lives and works from the land of the six Tewa Pueblos, located around the Rio Grande north of O'Ga P'Ogeh Owingeh, or present-day Santa Fe. For him and his people, the land is a sacred bounty. Vigil once tried to leave but was called back by the Clay Mother Spirit. Though his great-grandmother and great-aunts were potters, his relationship to clay was at first only peripheral; he quietly taught himself in secret, and this journey of self-discovery turned into an enriching lifelong pursuit.

Among the top awards at the Santa Fe Indian Art Market, Best in Show is perhaps the biggest honor for Native artists nationwide. These prizes are commemorated with ribbons that, for many, are far more prestigious than, for example, having work exhibited at the Metropolitan Museum of Art. Vigil has been bestowed both—a testament to the gift from his ancestors and the land.

—KR

Golden Clay Jar, 2008. Micaceous clay (full view and detail on p. 61)

Opposite: *Gourd Squash Blossom Style Jar*, c. 2011. Micaceous clay

Top: *Golden Fire Cloud Jar*, c. 2005. Micaceous clay

Bottom: *Undulated Gun Metal Gray Jar*, c. 2009. Micaceous clay

Mary Lee Hu

B. 1943, Lakewood, OH
Lives and works in Seattle, WA

Mary Lee Hu is a world traveler. The decision to lead with this descriptor instead of goldsmith, educator, weaver, or leader in the art jewelry field is purposeful to inform that she is first and foremost insatiably curious. In fact, her CV includes five pages of "Related Foreign Travel" outlining in thrilling detail her many trips and what she saw—from arctic animals, folk art museums, and silver markets to indigo dyers, floating villages, coppersmiths, and more. The more traditional sections of her resume tell you she's a "master" of her medium, has received multiple lifetime achievement awards, and was awarded the Smithsonian Visionary Award.

"Insatiable" is a descriptor that can also be applied to her chosen craft, the forthrightness of which she has been a lifetime devotee. At sixteen, Hu was introduced to metalworking and immediately decided it would be her future, but it wasn't until taking a weaving course during her MFA and assigned an off-loom project that it all clicked. Since then, she has expertly applied textile techniques to fine silver and high-carat gold wire, wrapping, knotting, braiding, knitting, and weaving it to create sumptuous, enveloping forms for the neck, ears, and hands. She favors neckpieces for their bigger scale, and her torques, chokers, and necklaces all somehow emulate a restrained opulence. "Fascinated by the whole range of body adornment through time and across cultures,"[1] Hu is a generous maker, her work figuratively translucent and sincere.

—KR

1 Mary Lee Hu, "Artist Statement" (unpublished manuscript, August 2023), Word document.

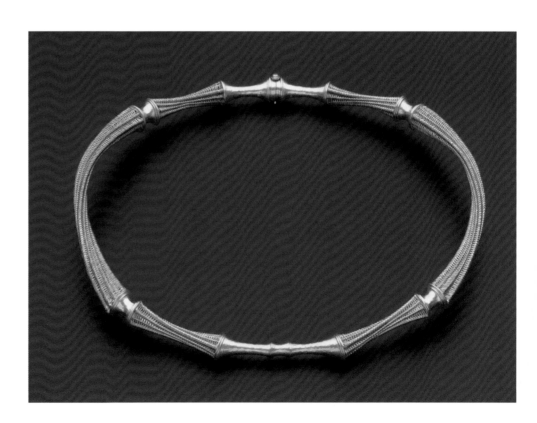

Choker #75, 1988. 18- and 22-karat gold

Opposite: *Choker #96*, 2021. 18- and 22-karat gold

Top: *Choker #90*, 2008. 18- and 22-karat gold (detail)

Bottom: Mary Lee Hu's living room with part of her jewelry library, 2023

Opposite: *Choker #78*, 1991. 18- and 22-karat gold

Ferne Jacobs

B. 1942, Chicago, IL
Lives and works in Los Angeles, CA

Since a life-changing workshop with artist Arline Fisch in the mid-1960s, Ferne Jacobs has dedicated over five decades to producing avant-garde fiber art. An early proponent of experimentation with natural fibers, she went off-loom to create organic and ethereal basket sculptures through a labor-intensive process of coiling waxed linen row by row. Jacobs animates these simple lines into fully fledged forms, accentuated by dynamic color play.

Her large-scale sculptures are seas of undulating lines that have no obvious point of origin or end, reflecting her intuitive process. Objects curve and sway with graceful movement as though they are dancing in the wind. She often turns basket weaving inside out, resulting in work that looks biological, such as wall works resembling cellular cross-sections of circulatory or skeletal systems, and in a less literal expression, the fluidity of emotions. After all, she says she wants to ensure that the work "feels alive, that it has breath."[1] Jacobs is a recipient of the Flintridge Foundation Award for Visual Artist (2005–6) and three National Endowment for the Arts Fellowships (1973, '77, '90). Her first retrospective exhibition, *Building the Essentials: Ferne Jacobs*, at the Craft in America Center, LA, took place in 2022.

—AVL

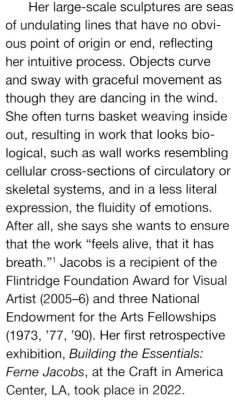

1 "Building the Essentials: Ferne Jacobs," Craft in America, accessed December 14, 2023, https://www.craftinamerica.org/exhibition/building-the-essentials-ferne-jacobs/.

Two Angels, 2015. Waxed linen thread

Opposite: *Interior Passages*, 2016. Waxed linen thread

Next pages: *Flight*, 2011. Waxed linen thread (detail)

Jamie Bennett

B. 1948, Philadelphia, PA
Lives and works in High Falls, NY
@bennettja

It is oddly puzzling to find the operative descriptor when it comes to Jamie Bennett, an enamelist who primarily works in art jewelry. His field's designations fail him, for he is also an abstractionist, a composer, a ponderer, and an educator who has transcended the material confines of his medium, as well as its historical and traditional connotations. Bennett's works teeter towards the realm of painting but are made in all dimensions. Rather than echo what many have already said about him, a keener statement to make would be that the "satisfying and still mystifying act"[1] of enamel is his domain entirely.

Through glass powder in every color expertly applied and fired, Bennett translates life's rhythms and curiosities into fantastical planes. The spectrum of his inspiration has ranged from the residual soot of a lit match to the many mediations of nature by humans, the result of which are magnified interpretations of pure color experiences, often fragmented into wearable, geometric polyptychs.

The time-consuming nature of his work always influenced the nurturing aspect of teaching, and vice versa. Bennett has also been in a classroom for the majority of his career and retired as professor emeritus at his alma mater SUNY (State University of New York) New Paltz, in 2014.

—KR

1   "Brilliance: Jamie Bennett," *American Craft*, September 8, 2013 (October/November 2013 issue), https://www.craftcouncil.org/magazine /article/brilliance-jamie-bennett.

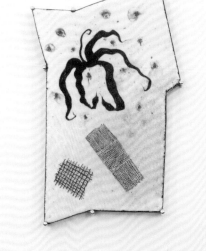

Ravenna No. 9 (Brooch), 2020. Enamel, stainless steel, and sterling silver (front and back)

Opposite: *In Aerem No. 11 (Necklace)*, 2019. Enamel and sterling silver

Top: *Poeticus*, 2023. Watercolor, gouache, ink, and gold leaf on Bristol paper

Bottom: Jamie Bennett's studio, 2023

Opposite: *Ravenna No. 11 (Brooch)*, 2021. Enamel, stainless steel, and sterling silver (front and back)

Bottom: *Ravenna No. 15 (Brooch)*, 2020. Enamel, stainless steel, and sterling silver

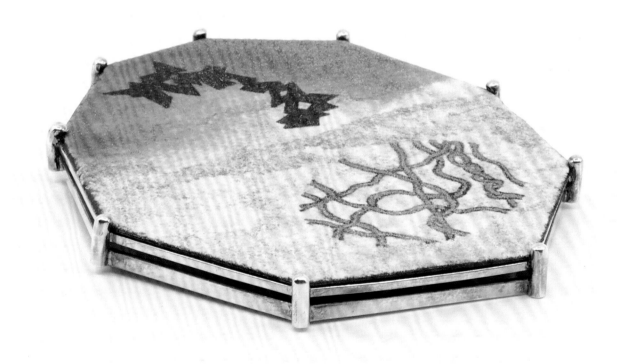

Jolie Ngo

B. 1996, Philadelphia, PA
Lives and works in Santa Barbara, CA
ngojolie.net
@jolienope

From Haystack to Santa Barbara, Jolie Ngo has crisscrossed the country in her car since completing her MFA from Alfred University in 2022. Residencies and teaching workshops are lifelines for young ceramic artists; the expense of acquiring a kiln of one's own is daunting, and thus the years after graduation are often nomadic. Most potters might keep their fettling knives and scrapers in a kit on the passenger seat. For Ngo, pride of place goes to her PotterBot 3D printer.

Ngo's work has been described as cyborgian, partly because of her use of modeling software to design forms and a robotic syringe to extrude clay. Ngo's landscapes are based on Minecraft and other video sandbox games, and her 2022 *Memory Palace* vessels often include digitally printed plastic signature bases in the shape of sneaker soles for extra Gen Z vibes.

In her recent work, the abrupt creative tension between the handmade and the digital has become nuanced, and her pieces have become more magisterial and reminiscent of 1950s abstract expressionist ceramics. Institutions have taken notice, with several of her largest-scale works to date acquired by the Everson Museum of Art in Syracuse, New York, and the Rhode Island School of Design Museum.

—JAMES ZEMAITIS

Flatpack Vessel in Dazzle Camo, 2023. Stoneware, glaze, and PVA plastic (bottom and side)

Opposite: *Stacked Flat*, 2020. Terra-cotta, terra sigillata, and glaze

Next pages: *Flatpack Vessel in Wavy*, 2023. Stoneware and glaze

Vincent Pocsik

B. 1985, Cleveland, OH
Lives and works in Los Angeles, CA
vincentpocsik.com
@vincentpocsik

Vincent Pocsik's giants reflect the trichotomy of man, machine, and nature. Sometimes they are at odds with one another; other times, in harmony. It is this tension that influences Pocsik's sculptural furniture—the supernatural, sometimes grotesque anatomies that emerge are caught in the ongoing negotiation of dominance between these three elements. Nature is still calming and seductively provocative to this city-kid designer, which he says he cannot hope to replicate; wood remains Pocsiks's material of choice because it is beautiful to begin with.

When designing his forms, Pocsik starts with a sketch and then uses an animation software he learned in architecture school to augment the designs, which get sent to a CNC machine to be cut in blocks, and then assembled and finished by hand. Though the designer leaves traces of the mill bit on the surface of the wood, he does not want the digital fabrication component to be fetishized. Rather, it is the underlaying and overlaying of all different inputs that make the work singular. Pocsik has no immediate plans to disrupt this process and feels he is just digging into his visual language. "Diligence is important. The lamps are growing, and I'm learning about them. They are characters and aliens trying to figure out the metaphysical idea of being. When you focus on something for a really long time, it becomes part of you."[1]

—KR

---

1 Vincent Pocsik, interview by Kellie Riggs, September 29, 2023.

Yard Play, 2022. Bleached black walnut

Opposite: *Bodies Chant Electric: Sitting with One Rain Boot in Cherry*, 2023. Cherry, resin, and lighting elements

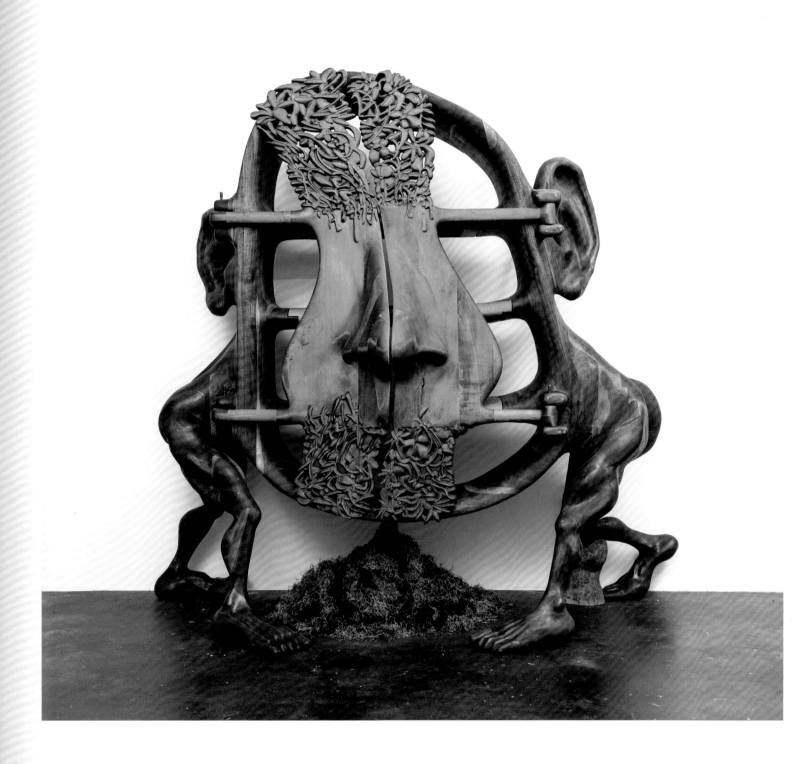

Cabinet Is Me, 2022. Dyed black walnut and maple

Opposite, left: Vincent Pocsik in his studio, 2023

Right: *From This Within*, 2023. Black walnut

Mallory Weston

B. 1986, Edison, NJ
Lives and works in Philadelphia, PA
malloryweston.com
@_mallory_weston_

Mallory Weston's jewelry captures the beauty of nature with a futuristic edge. The metallic leaves she makes as ornaments recall the shine of the sleek mobile devices in our hands, an analogy for the virality and propagation of information on the cybernetic landscape. While her jewelry undeniably draws from internet aesthetics, it stems from a hybrid approach combining analog processes with computer-aided design.

The former approach includes stitching small pieces of metal together by hand for a pixelated surface and re-creating the colors and patterns of popular tropical plants with precision by anodizing titanium. The soft joints between metal bits give the work an unexpected flexibility that follows in the tradition of celebrated artists like Arline Fisch and Mary Lee Hu, known for weaving metal jewelry.

In employing symbols of our digital culture, Weston reflects on the appeal of interactions on social media platforms. The works' abundance of "wormhole" cavities—features that would be impossible to create without digital design tools—are not dissimilar from cameras on phones or peepholes, underscoring our society's voyeuristic tendencies. Weston's unlikely pairing of botany and technology is a critical exploration of the human desire for connection.

—AVL

Anthurium Wormhole Necklace #1, 2021.
Anodized titanium, leather, polyester, and cotton

Opposite: *Op Selloum Brooch #1*, 2022.
Anodized titanium, brass, nickel, leather, cotton, and powder coat

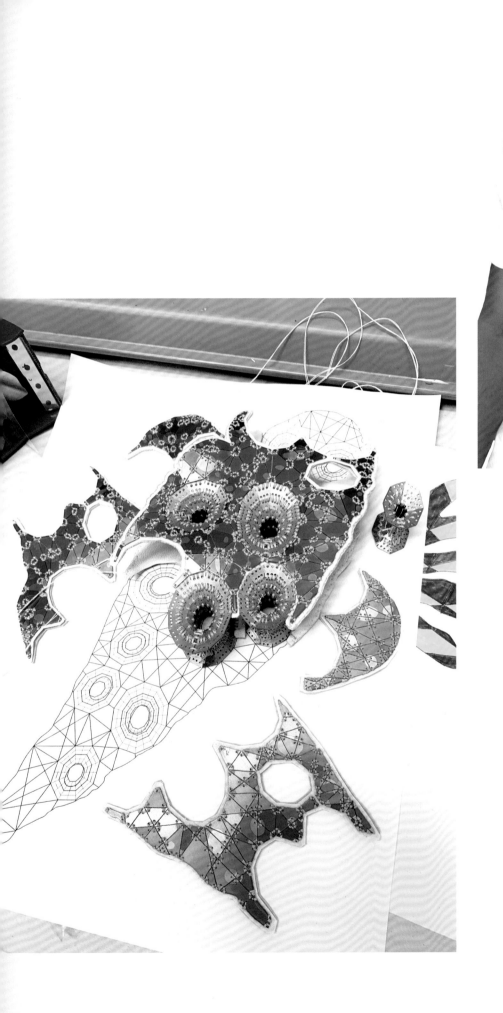

Maculata Wormhole Necklace #1, 2022. Anodized titanium, leather, and cotton

Opposite: *Romantic Subjects*, 2023. Anodized titanium, leather, and cotton. Helen M. Danforth Acquisition Fund 2023.124, Museum of Art, Rhode Island School of Design (detail and full view on p. 82)

Matthew Szösz

B. 1974, Providence, RI
Lives and works in Seattle, WA
matthewszosz.com
@c.matthewszosz

Technical prowess meets a punk attitude in Matthew Szösz's ongoing exploration of the limits of glass. Although he gained greater control as he developed his *Inflatables* series over fifteen years, the process remains an investigation within the pursuit of surprising others and himself. To create these pieces, Szösz first cuts salvaged or found window glass into a desired shape and stacks the resulting sheets between layers of ceramic fiber paper to prevent fusion. When he applies heat to the stacked sheets, a cavity forms between them through which he pumps compressed air and inflates the glass. The form puffs, cools, and solidifies in seconds, as if like magic. This process allows him to work without a team, which goes against typical blown glass practices.

Each *Inflatable* results from a collaboration between the material, physics, and Szösz's careful engineering. Simple two-dimensional shapes become complex compositions with exoskeletons and engorged bodies, with recent versions made of metal-coated iridized glass that appear extra-terrestrial. Other experimentations using commonplace machinery (as opposed to high-tech digital tools) include making glass lace to underscore the material's inherent fragility and fluidity and weaving sculptures out of glass rope.

—AVL

untitled(inflatable)no. 100bir, 2022. Glass

Opposite: *untitled(inflatable)no. 39*, 2008. Glass

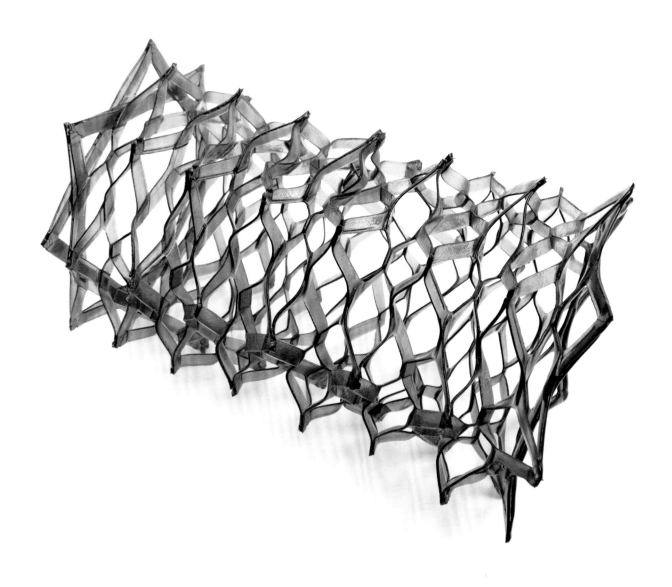

Opposite: *Euplectella*, 2022. Digital video (stills)

This page, top: *Retiarius*, 2014. Glass

Bottom: *untitled(inflatable)no. 91b*, 2019. Glass

Joyce Lin

B. 1994, Durham, NC
Lives and works in Houston, TX
joyce-lin.com
@jolime

For *Material Autopsy*, her 2023 solo exhibition at R & Company, Joyce Lin astonished collectors and curators with two seminal chair designs that epitomized her cerebral, forensic approach to woodworking. Her *Root Chair* is a variation from a series originally commissioned by the New Orleans Museum of Art, when Lin visited the vanishing wetlands of Louisiana. There she was deeply moved by the "ghost forests," where cedar stands have been destroyed by brackish water flowing into the marshes, a result of human interference in the ecosystem and climate change. This led to her gathering driftwood from the Brazos River in Texas and the Mississippi River in New Orleans, burning the silhouette of a vernacular ladderback chair into the assembled limbs and, in Lin's words, "finding a kind of sublime beauty within destruction and loss."[1]

In contrast, Lin's *Wood Chair* is all subterfuge and artifice, wherein the actual plywood structure is hidden under layers of epoxy clay and paint. After intense studies of grain and bark, Lin sculpts her tribute to a species—oak, fir, walnut, ash—in a series that has been acquired by several museums, including Munson in Utica, New York, and the Carnegie Museum of Art in Pittsburgh, Pennsylvania. Field research and scientific method are engrained in Lin's practice (she received dual degrees from Rhode Island School of Design and Brown University in Furniture Design and Geology-Biology), and she accompanies each design with detailed drawings and descriptions.

—JZ

"Object Lesson: An Interview with Designer Joyce Lin," New Orleans Museum of Art, December 7, 2022, https://noma.org/joyce-lin-interview/.

Wood, Metal, Stone, 2023. Wood, MDF, paint, stain, and steel

Opposite: *Wood Chair*, 2023. Wood, MDF, epoxy clay, and paint

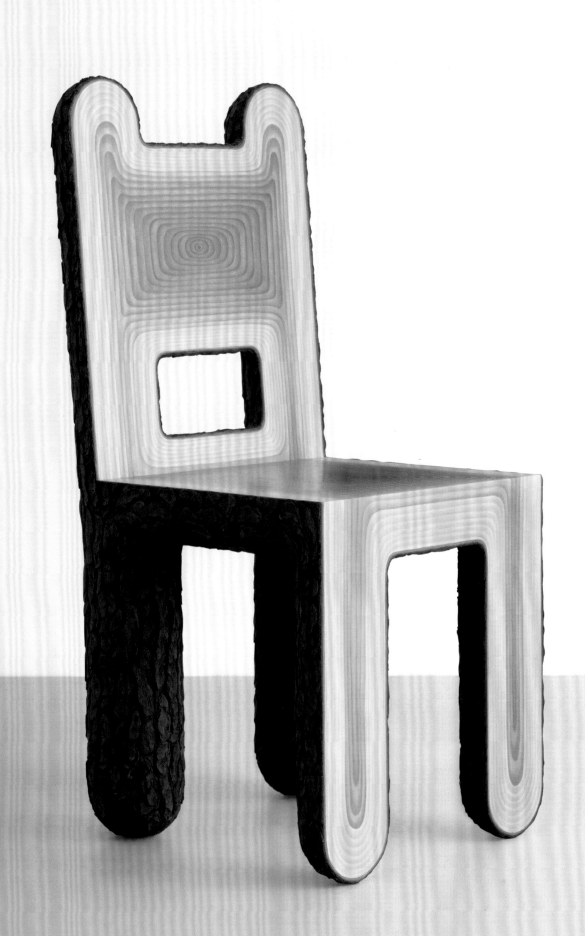

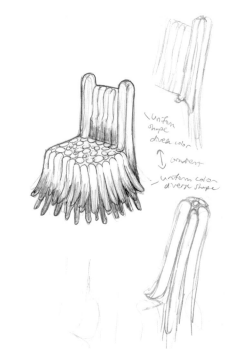

Clockwise from top left: Sketches at Joyce Lin's studio, 2023; sketch for *Root Chair*, 2023; detail from *Root Chair*; Lin picking wood from the Brazos River mouth, 2022

Opposite: *Root Chair*, 2023. Driftwood and stain

Brian Oakes

B. 1995, Harrington Park, NJ
Lives and works in Brooklyn, NY
brianoakes.xyz
@broakes

Though we are dependent on the electrical components that go into our devices, most people know and care little about them. Not Brian Oakes, who considers circuit boards a "hyper contemporary object that could never have been before."[1] Their interest in electronics was solidified in art school, where they were a sculpture major with a concentration in Computation, Technology, and Culture. At first, the designer elected to make their own circuit boards by hand, but designing them and having them manufactured made the operation repeatable and scalable. Now, to develop the aggressive-looking board shapes, they utilize the surrealist tradition of automatic drawing and then scans them into a computer. Oakes's multiplying forms have become far more complex, free-standing objects.

Using cyber-gothic industrial vocabularies, the dynamic lighted structures are programmed to a sequence that has them blink in many colors to display what the artist calls "functional states of chaos in the most ambient way possible."[2] Pieces like *Vessel 1* additionally employ motorized elements that move up and down. Oakes has also experimented with numbered channel systems that randomly record the surrounding ambient noise so their creatures can play it back to give their work more humanoid qualities, simulating twitching or breathing. The chaotic-neutral sci-fi-fantasy objects are intensified by an abundance of power cords—another raw material of the future—giving the concept of structure as form in art-making an entirely new meaning.

—KR

---

1 Brian Oakes, email message to Kellie Riggs, December 1, 2023.
2 Oakes, email.

Mimesis System 8, 2022. Printed circuit boards, electronic components, microphones, audio cables, power supply, chain, and miscellaneous hardware

Opposite: *Mimesis System 6 Prime*, 2021. Printed circuit boards, electronic components, microphones, audio cables, power supply, aluminum extrusion, and miscellaneous hardware

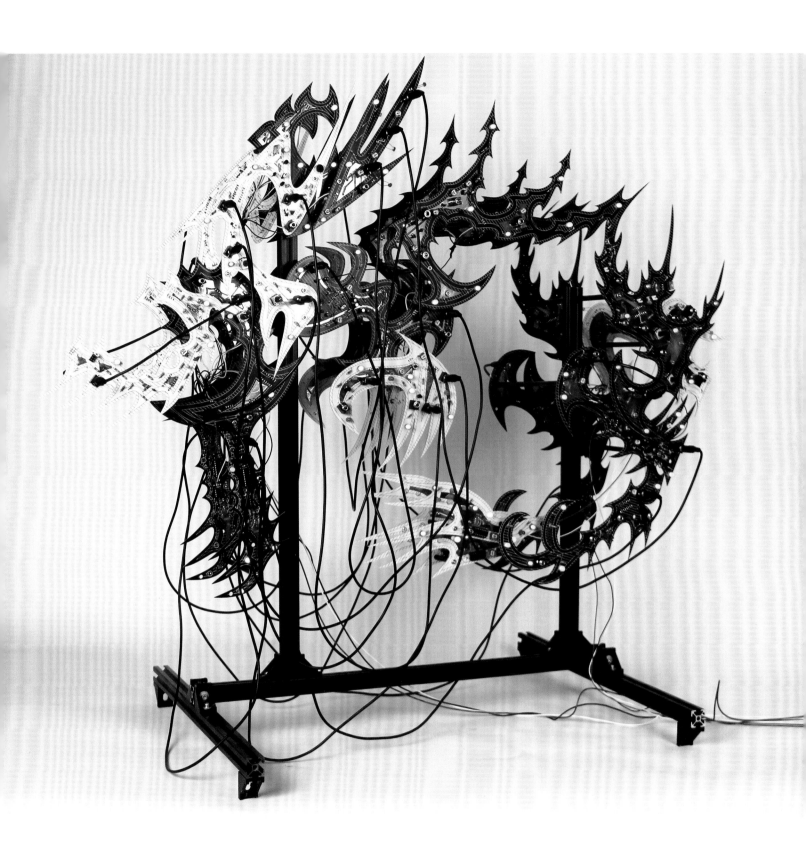

Opposite, top and bottom left: Brian Oakes working on *Vessel 1* (full view on p. 25)

Bottom right: *Control System 3 (Sconce)* in progress, 2023

Installation view of *America Runs* at Dunkunsthalle, 2023

Adam Grinovich

B. 1981, Beverly, MA
Lives and works in Warren, VT, and Penland, SC
adamgrinovich.com
@adamgrinovich

Adam Grinovich liberates his jewelry by doubling down on its archetypes to create frenetic, overzealous remixes. Taking cues from luxury markets and the absurdity of collab culture—with the augmented amalgamations that come with it—he transfers that hyperness to a field that tends to feel stuck in the past: art jewelry.

During a 2014 residency at a 3D-printing company specializing in bone and dental implants, he was the first in his niche to use the technology to print directly in stainless steel. Grinovich's designs exploited the interdependent structural scaffolding needed for a successful print by aestheticizing it even further in the design process (versus removing it entirely), thereby showcasing it within the final form. This is the case for *Ziggurat*,

which is finished with comically large cubic zirconia.

After a hiatus due to a five-year teaching appointment at Savannah College of Art and Design, the jeweler started using materials like nylon and other synthetics found in footwear to poke fun at the capitalist zeitgeist that has us scrambling to look cool and fit in but remain unique at the same time. Rooted in his success as a bushcrafter in the jewelry world, his practice also questions whether something "new" is no longer new at all. After all, now talent and expertise are largely determined by the resourcefulness with which we excavate the Anthropocene that our insatiable consumerist habits helped create.

—KR

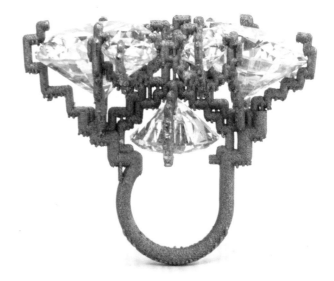

Ziggurat, 2016. Stainless steel and cubic zirconia

Opposite: *Armored Core 1*, 2023. Sterling silver, brass, nylon, resin, and cubic zirconia

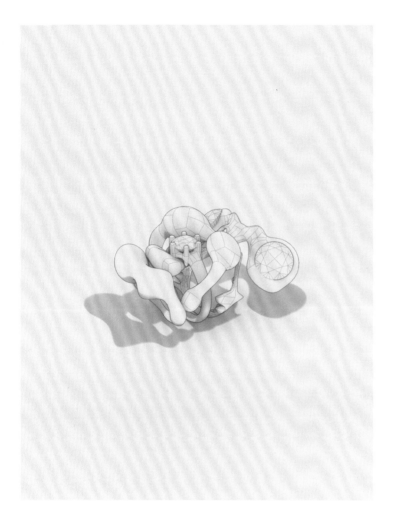

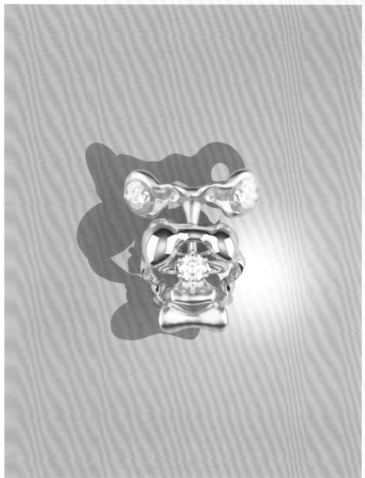

Top, left and right: Digital drawings for the
Armored Core series, 2023

Opposite: *Tropical Space*, 2017. Stainless steel,
cubic zirconia, and paracord

Layla Klinger

B. 1993, Tel Aviv
Lives and works in Brooklyn, NY
laylank.com
@violetmenace

"Physical computing" is how Layla Klinger refers to their practice of scaling up structures found in textiles and illuminating them with touch-sensitive electrical currents. Tension is both the subject and the system holding together their sculptures. Klinger is a self-taught bobbin lace maker who applies their interest and experiences in coding to create immersive, life-size, color-changing installations made from electroluminescent wire, a material they encountered during their time at electronic textile camp in 2023. The complexities of the works also reflect the erotic queer spaces important to the artist, where bodies are encouraged to touch, explore, and see what happens—and where object and subject are one and the same. To experience their work, you have to be a part of it, so Klinger wants the viewer to come down to the lace's level, which in essence, is constituted by holes. In speaking about *Pollination*, "On one hand it's erotic, and on the other it is violent; it's a still object constantly committed to being touched."[1] When activated, Klinger's work aims to signify positive or negative touch, consent or displeasure, through light; and the entanglement of the work itself is analogous to queer "safe spaces" that the artist feels are both liberating and confining at the very same time.

—KR

1   Layla Klinger, interview by Kellie Riggs, October 4, 2023.

Follow You in Roses, 2023. Electroluminescent wire

Opposite: *Infinite Pollination (Torchon 01)*, 2023. Electroluminescent wire, wrapping wire, LDR sensors, and EL Sequencer

Next pages, left: *Infinite Pollination (Rose 01)*, 2022. Electroluminescent wire, wrapping wire, LDR sensors, and EL Sequencer (stills from the activation)

Top right: *Still, Missing You (C'mon Everybody)*, 2021. Electroluminescent wire (detail)

Bottom right: Installation view of *Hot House* at Houston Center for Contemporary Craft, 2023

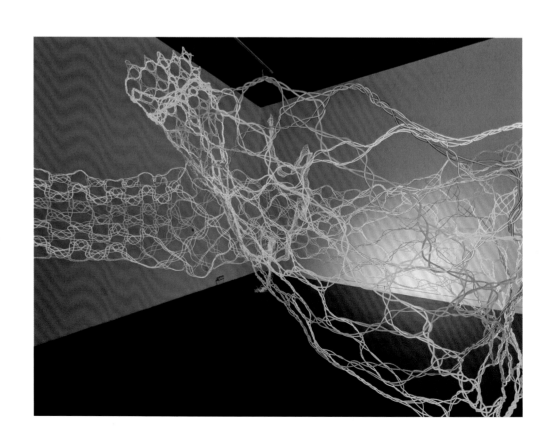

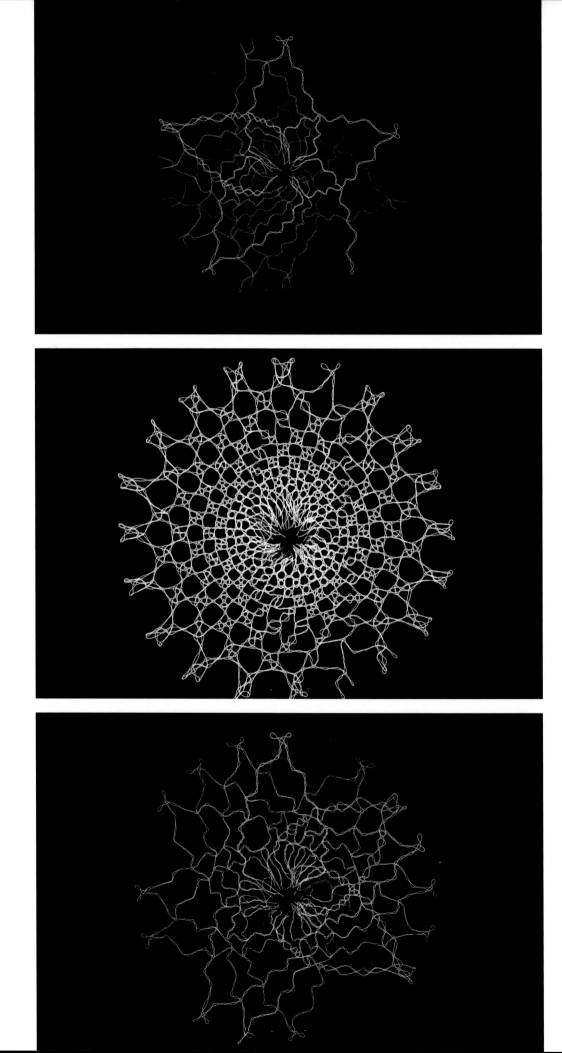

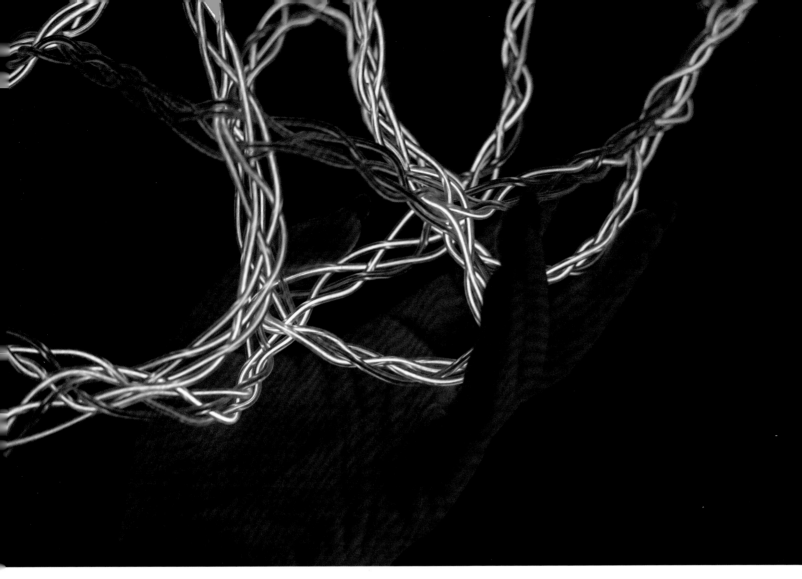

Georgina Treviño

B. 1989, San Diego, CA
Lives and works in San Diego, CA
georginatrevinojewelry.com
@georginatrevino

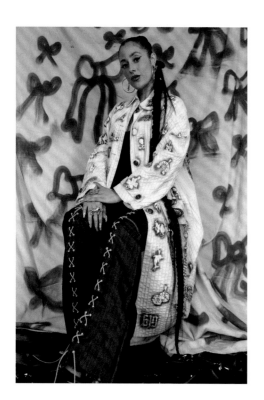

Anything can be jewelry in Georgina Treviño's shiny universe—a crushed soda can, a park bench, cutlery, and more. She uses the lens of jewelry to make wearables and sculptures that do away with the preciousness often ascribed to the medium. Growing up between San Diego and Tijuana, she struggled to define her identity until she became immersed in the burgeoning fashion scene of Mexico, an evident influence in her fashion-forward work.

With a finger always on the pulse of what is relevant, she stamps, pierces, and casts elements of American and Latine pop culture and Y2K nostalgia into her sought-after pieces, which have been worn by the hottest pop stars. Treviño's work often features direct and bold statements that reveal something about the wearer's identity or that command an action, expanding the long tradition of the nameplate. Although metal is her primary material, in the artist's nonhierarchical creative approach, she combines handmade components with mass-produced items such as keys or old CDs to give new life to what many would call trash. Treviño elevates the materials into coveted items without obscuring their raw state and humble origins.

—AVL

La Vida es Como un Columpio, 2023. Stainless steel

Opposite: *Norteña*, 2023. Upcycled purse and belt buckles

Top: *10-4 Compa!*, 2023. Sterling silver, phone charger, and flip phone

Bottom: *No Scrubs*, 2021. CD and zirconia

Opposite: *Culona Frikitona*, 2023. Steel and stainless steel

Lilah Rose

B. 1990, Rockford, MI
Lives and works in Los Angeles, CA
lilahslagerrose.com
@lilahslagerrose

A battle between codependency and obsolescence has always been present in the automobile industry, especially in places like Detroit and Los Angeles. The former is artist Lilah Rose's home state, and the latter where she is based now. The investment into a vehicle is personal, often one of means, comfort, or status, never financial, and hardly environmental. For about five years, Rose has been transmuting her lifelong fascination with cars into soft, sculptural wall reliefs to tease out humans' conflicted relationship with them. With names like *Citroën Canyon* and *Corvetticus,* her works are rendered plush, silky, and colorful and often look like quilts, comforters, or mattresses embellished with stacked, piled, multiplying, or splitting car bodies. The cartoony yet tailored figures are commentaries but also tributes, their sensual but tension-filled

forms a nod to the classic, well-crafted cars of generations past.

Other work by Rose depicts personal, fragmented dreamscapes reminiscent of architecture, memories, and nostalgia. When making the quilted, hand-dyed works, some come together quickly, while others test her patience. There is no formula, no reliable results. Not unlike the eventual, fossilized detritus of cars that can no longer run, her pieces aim to create an "endless time loop—a memory that exists forever."[1]

—KR

---

1 Lilah Rose, in Art Alerts (formerly David The Collector), "Artist Interview with Lilah Rose - Explore The Meaning Behind Her Soft Sculptures At New Image Art," YouTube, February 28, 2022, https://www.youtube.com/watch?v=BF3RI15ktIs.

Evil Nineoneones, 2024. Cotton and satin

Opposite: *Jeanette*, 2021. Muslin, poly-fil, satin, fabric dye, and acrylic

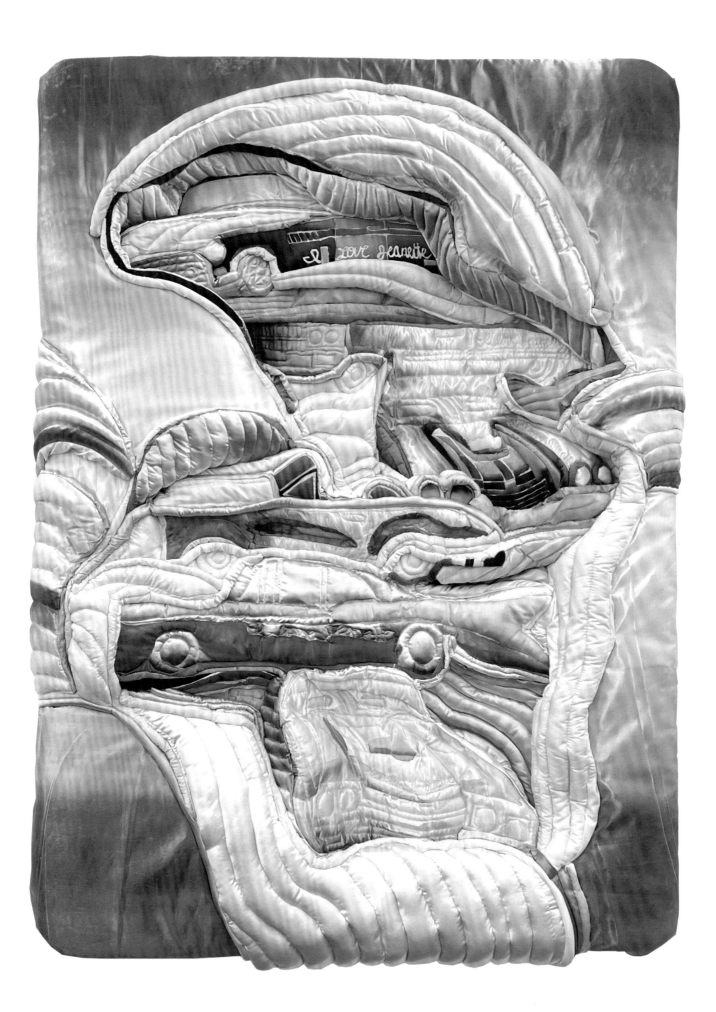

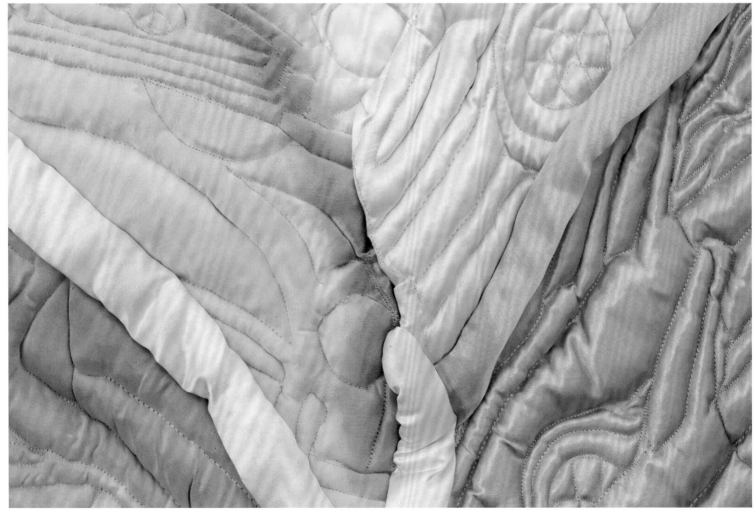

Opposite, top: Lilah Rose working on a small abstract sculpture in satin and cotton

Opposite, bottom and this page, left: *Delta*, 2022. Satin, cotton, fabric dye, and acrylic on wood

Right: *Oil Ride*, 2021. Foam, satin, and fabric dye over wood board

Ryan Decker

B. 1997, Cape Coral, FL
Lives and works in Brooklyn, NY
rydeck.com
@ry.deck

In Ryan Decker's furniture, sculpture, animation, and digital paintings, the tangible and intangible collide. His objects live somewhere between the physical and the virtual—these two planes constantly perused, confused, and infused. This refers to more than just his making process, which happens primarily in VR, but also to the sources of his creations and even the destination, which are taken from the playbook of MMORPGs (massively multiplayer online role-playing games).

Decker's 2022 hyper-lamps like *Sluggard Waker* utilize a future-medieval trompe l'oeil that takes flat sheets of printed aluminum into the round. Boggling to look at, these pieces disrupt our perception of them, even in the flesh; the brain simply cannot keep up with their changing dimensionality. The same can be said about images of his exhibition *Feudal Relief* from the same year, where 3D works in wood and bronze appear to be props in a cluttered video game still, but one that was brought to an impossibly high resolution. A mischievous charcuterie board outfitted with a CD drive or a poster display stand exhibiting surrealist landscapes are other bizarre propositions. Are they the prizes we work towards in a simulation, or goofy mockeries to the collective lives we live exceptionally online? In and of itself, Decker's whole practice is a fantastical, immersive exercise in "alternativism"—not better or worse than our current moment in society, but a self-referential something else entirely.

—KR

Dwellings for Ruffled Warblers, 2022. UV-printed aluminum composite, polylactic acid, acrylic, and full-range speakers

Opposite: *Sluggard Waker*, 2023. UV-printed aluminum composite, polylactic acid, hydrographic film, acrylic, lamp parts

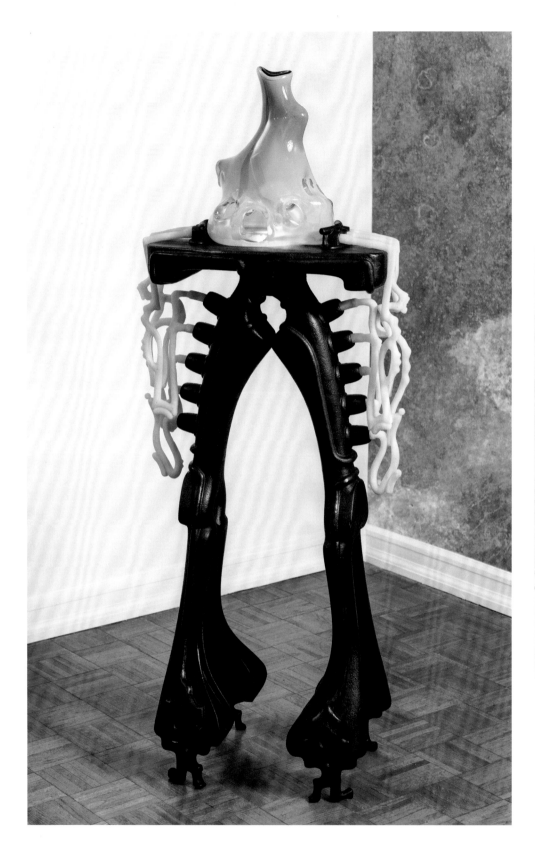

Left: *Bionic Knees for Atlas*, 2021. Cast iron, blown glass, silicone, and lamp parts

Right: *Lantern for Your Downtown Dungeon*, 2022. UV-printed aluminum, cast glass, and lamp parts (detail)

Opposite: Installation view of *Feudal Relief* at Superhouse, 2022

Amia Yokoyama

B. Illinois
Lives and works in Los Angeles, CA
amiayokoyama.com
@amiayokoyama

Amia Yokoyama operates as a material hacker, rejecting linear constructs of reality. Instead, she concentrates on world-building with porcelain sculptures and digital manipulations that embrace the genesis of alternative realities through multiplicity, glitches, and fantasy. The gooey quality of her work represents the concept of flux, a continuous regeneration of matter, time, and context, where a lump of clay can become a body, and a body can become a lump of clay in an eternal cycle.

Yokoyama's recurrent watery femme figures are metaphorical "clay bodies" inspired by the limitless worlds of anime and manga. They serve as avatars that unbound the spirit from the confines of a physical body subjected to fetishization. She uses porcelain explicitly because it is a historically and politically charged symbol of desire and commodification and as an entry point into her Japanese heritage, where the material problematically represents Asian femininity.

A new series of works comprising wall-mounted obsidian plaques become portals into another dimension inhabited by her clay avatars printed as holograms. The objects are anachronistic, with sleek "black mirrors" revealing *Matrix*-green images housed within earthy porcelain frames that do not attempt to hide the artist's hand.

—AVL

Abound, 2022–23. Porcelain, stoneware, and glaze

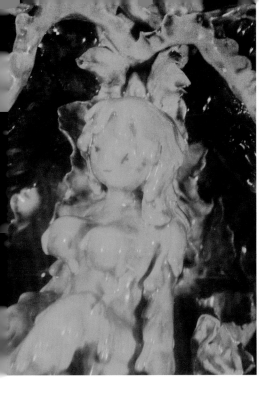

Opposite, left: *Tower (Accumulation)*, 2022–23. Porcelain, stoneware, and glaze

Center: Amia Yokoyama's studio, 2023

This page, top: *Mirror 1 / Glint*, 2022–23. Ceramic, glass, obsidian, pumice stone, holographic print, and wood (detail)

Right: *Mirror 2 / Entanglement*, 2022–23. Ceramic, glass, holographic print, obsidian, and wood

Sulo Bee

B. 1993, San Antonio, TX
Lives and works in San Antonio, TX
sparklefilth.cloud
@sparkle_filth

Through their jewelry practice, Sulo Bee is developing a new visual language tuned into nonbinary existence. The lexicon comes from a nirvana-like space caught between the social and material binaries called "$P4RKL3_FiLTH_CL0UD_NiN3", which Bee found after receiving gender-affirming top surgery. Able to better relate to their body and the jewelry they make, Bee started to see the world with new eyes, turning to nature for inspiration. Their large-scale yet lightweight neckpieces, pendants, and bolo ties are glyphs within an experimental queer lexicon.

The artist makes human-made detritus appear organic with blobby shapes achieved through various techniques, including electroforming, hammering, hollow forming, and patinated and spray-painted surfaces. The work is "equal parts sparkle and filth," according to Bee.[1] Engraved with blind contour drawings of natural elements and titles featuring a medley of numbers, letters, and symbols akin to internet usernames, Bee's jewelry functions as a futuristic cuneiform free from binaries. The experimental quality of their work is a reflection of their ever-evolving nonbinary identity. Bee is also the co-founder of Queer Metalsmiths, an organization with the mission of uplifting queer voices in the fields of metalsmithing and craft.

—AVL

---

1 Sulo Bee, "Artist Statement," $P4RKL3_FiLTH, December 14, 2023, https://www.sparklefilth .cloud/about.

GHUZN00LZ[GL00MLURK3R], 2023. Copper, brass, silver, shell, rough uncut diamonds, rubber, stickers, glitter, and paint

Opposite, left: *D0_U_B3Li3V3_iN_M3*, 2022. Copper, brass, steel, silver, shell, rubber, stickers, glitter, and paint

Right: *$P4CEC0W[bb]_DR3AMZ*, 2024. Steel, copper, silver, geodes rubber, epoxy, and paint

Clockwise from top left: Sulo Bee soldering hollow forms and electroformed components; making *C4ZP4RZ_B3Z3RK3R*; sketching in the studio; decorating with sgraffito on painted surfaces

Opposite: *C4ZP4RZ_B3Z3RK3R*, 2023. Steel, fine silver, sterling silver, copper, spray paint, epoxy, stickers, glitter, and rubber

Chen Chen & Kai Williams

B. 1985, Shanghai, China; B. 1984, New York, NY
Live and work in Brooklyn, NY
cckw.us
@chenandkai

Design studio Chen Chen & Kai Williams takes samples of our natural world and present them as conserved specimens. Set like gemstones to be maintained for a mineral-stripped future, their *Geology* and *Transition* series have an artifactual air as though they will soon be no longer. In their twelve years together, Chen and Williams have maintained a straightforward "do with what you have" type of approach. Valuing the transformative abilities of both natural and industrial materials has been a huge part of their ongoing investigation as makers. Within the context of shifting material values in a planet subject to continued depletion of natural resources and rare earth elements, their output seems cleverly ad hoc. In the past they've cast aluminum into water, zinc onto glass, and turned used plastic shopping bags into a form-giving material.

Chen and Williams's work is inventive yet direct. Absent of any pretense, their descriptions are written as a play by play of how the thing was made. Fundamental information remains open-source. This spirit is confirmed by the Archive section of their website, which is set up as a convincing dupe of Wikipedia—the history of each piece, its process, its material DNA all there with the click of a hyperlink. Their practice-as-data advances perhaps arbitrary but mesmerizing knowledge, setting their work up to be recovered no matter what the future holds.

—KR

Geology Table 03, 2018. Stone and steel

Opposite: *Transition Mirror No. 1*, 2019. Stone, glass, and steel

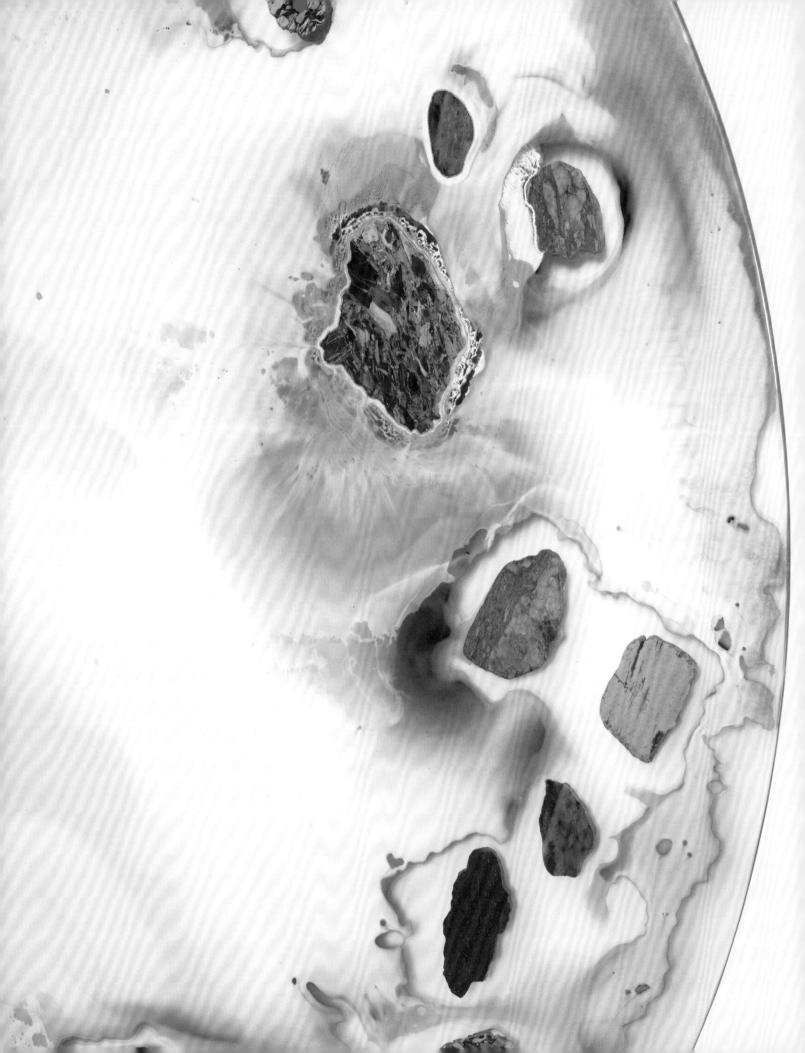

Opposite: *Transition Mirror 2021–6001*, 2021.
Stone, glass, and steel (detail)

Installation view of *Romancing the Stone* at
Casa Perfect New York, 2019

Cammie Staros

B. 1983, Nashville, TN
Lives and works in Los Angeles, CA
cammiestaros.com
@cammiestaros

Over the last decade, Cammie Staros has investigated how Greco-Roman artifacts came to represent a point of origin for Western art history. Her sculptures are hybrids of antiquity and modern industry, with their display format playing an essential role in their conceptual framework. She primarily engages the language of the vessel, which she warps into unconventional forms and augments with spider webs made of metal chains, neon light attachments, and floating plexiglass pedestals.

Staros's work foreshadows what might become of prized objects in the future and how they will shape the understanding of our legacy, as ceramic remnants have done for past civilizations. Fish tanks make for an unpredictable presentation case for her vessels, establishing an unfixed timeline between ancient shipwrecks and archeological ruins of a post-apocalyptic future reeling from an ecological disaster. Staros manipulates the forms of the submerged vessels to exaggerate the distortion caused by their aqueous habitats. Often inhabited by fish and plants, the watery containers posit a hypothetical future in which museological displays have fallen into abandonment as the natural environment reclaims objects that were once organic. Her practice considers how shifting context can create new meanings and alternative narratives.

—AVL

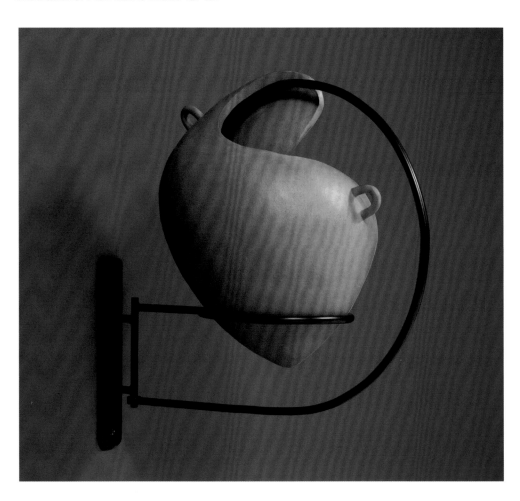

Reditus naturalis, 2022. Ceramic and steel

Opposite: *Piscina reflexionis*, 2022. Ceramic, acrylic, wood, laminate, steel, water, aquatic filtration system, grow light, and seiryu stone

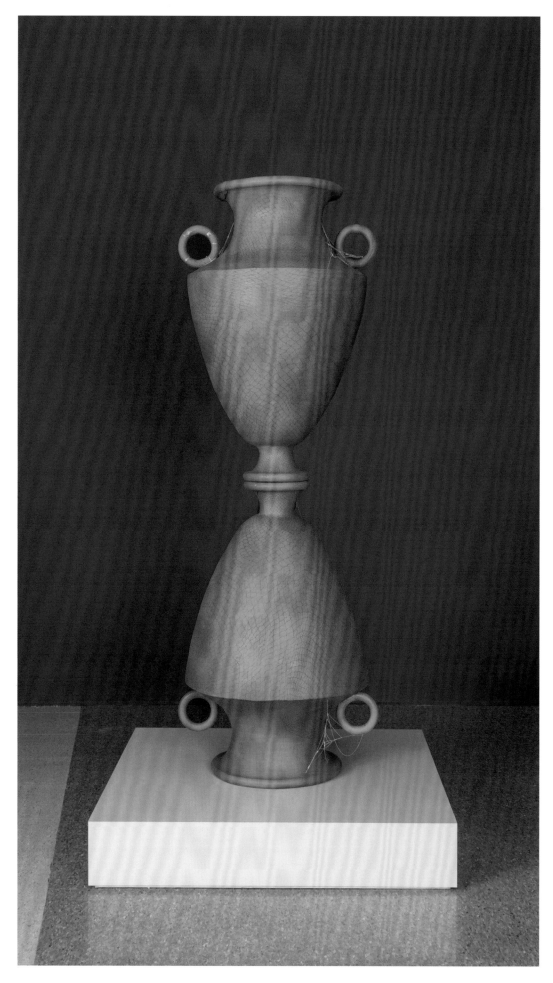

Opposite: *Net of Hephaestus*, 2022. Ceramic and silver

Left, top and bottom: *Sculptura liquefacta*, 2021. Ceramic, acrylic, wood, laminate, water, aquatic filtration system, programmed grow light, river rock, Japanese ohko stone, and aquatic plants

Right: *Face of Athena, Back of Man and Beast*, 2023. Ceramic, pebbles, and shells

MJ Tyson

B. 1986, Morristown, NJ
Lives and works in Morristown, NJ
mjtyson.com
@mj_tyson

A contemporary take on memento mori jewelry—reminders of the inevitability of death—MJ Tyson's sculptural vessels and jewelry are composites of forsaken metal objects, which she melts and combines with the potential to hold new meaning for others. Old coins, watches, and silverware are among the items she chooses to freeze in flux as memorials for the people, living or deceased, who left them behind. Her work marks the fleeting nature of human life and the reincarnation of material things.

Invested in how objects serve as containers of memory, she displays each of her jewelry pieces in a velvet-lined box that holds the impression of the object and, therefore, its memory, even when the object is removed. Among the compacted strata of pooling iron, gold, silver, and copper in her sculptures, one can glimpse the ornate edge of a plate or a number from a license plate, a hint of their past lives. While Tyson's process may come across to some as a twisted fate, it is a practical alternative for objects that may be outdated or no longer hold value. Her reconstituted sculptures and jewelry are sentimental markers of a place or person's story.

—AVL

Left: MJ Tyson melting personal objects

Right: Casting in process

Opposite: *35 Norman Avenue*, 2019. Personal objects left behind by the deceased residents of 35 Norman Avenue

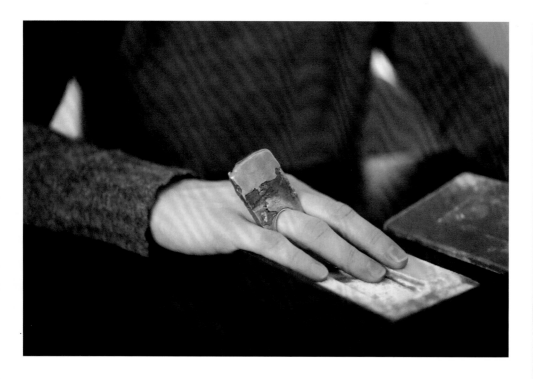

Left, top and bottom: *Dust to Dust*, 2018.
Reconstituted jewelry in velvet box

Right: *145 Delmage Road* (2017), *61 High Street*
(2018), *52 Underwood Street* (2017), *102 Garden
Hills Drive* (2017), *80 Church Street* (2017).
Personal objects left behind by the deceased
residents of these homes

Myra Mimlitsch-Gray

B. 1962, Camden, NJ
Lives and works in Stone Ridge, NY
mimlitschgray.com
@mimgray

A virtuoso in the art of metalsmithing and holloware, Myra Mimlitsch-Gray is a national treasure who also makes treasures. She goes beyond giving family heirlooms superficial facelifts by starting from scratch—her intuitive interpretations of candleholders and serving trays are raised by hand from sheets of metal with the expert, repetitive blow of the hammer. By pushing the periodic elements to their sensual and theatrical extremes, she gives her objects an agency that their dated relatives simply did not have.

Over the course of her starred career, results have defied themselves in a myriad of ways. Mimlitsch-Gray's pieces may posture as historic or didactic, but they are caught in the act of splitting, melting, puffing, being torn or squished—all while earnestly attempting to get away from themselves, to move on from where they have always been placed. But her objects show this is only possible to a degree. The material imposition inherent to them comes with baggage: silver is "eternally challenging, both a joy and a bitch to work with. Brass is, well, brassy—annoying and brash—that's what I like about it. Bronze has honorific, commemorative, and statuary connotations, which I work with."[1] The legacies, hierarchies, and problems connected to class, utility, and service are similarly impossible to ignore. Liking metal even for all its difficulties, she works through her gut reactions to storied objects with a prowess that borders on the unbelievable.

—KR

1 Myra Mimlitsch-Gray, interview by Kellie Riggs, September 21, 2023.

The Flap, 2014. Porcelain enamel on steel

Opposite: *Party Barge*, 2024. Sterling silver
(top and bottom)

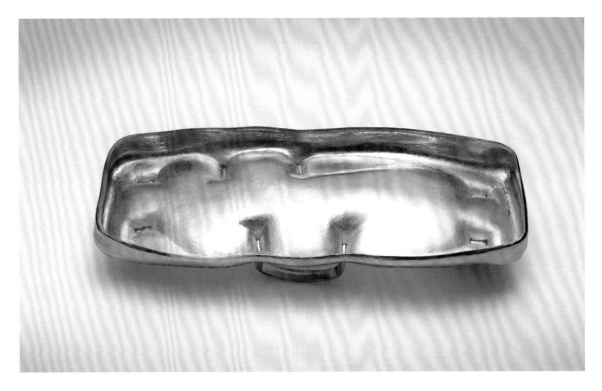

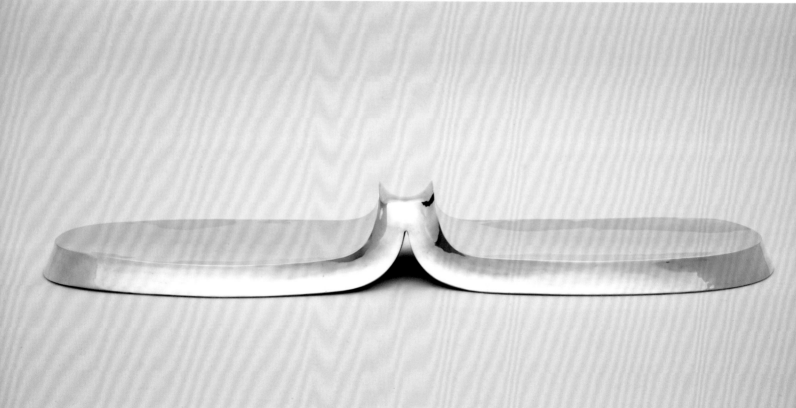

Top: Myra Mimlitsch-Gray in her studio forming a copper vessel, 2023

Bottom: *Split Slab*, 2020. Silver. The Museum of Fine Arts, Houston, museum purchase funded by the GRITS Foundation and the Art Colony Association, Inc., 2017.234

Top: Installation view of *Prima Materia: The Periodic Table in Contemporary Art* at the Aldrich Contemporary Art Museum, 2023

Bottom: *Red and White Pitcher*, 2014. Enamel on steel

Francesca DiMattio

B. 1981, New York, NY
Lives and works in New York, NY
@francescadimattio

More is more when it comes to Francesca DiMattio. Her approach to making is as excessive and theatrical as the Rococo style she often alludes to in her sculptures and furniture. As an ancient discipline, ceramics have a vast catalog of styles to draw from by today's artists engaging in the medium—as is the case for DiMattio, whose passion for historical references also manifests through nods to British Wedgwood, Greek black-and-red-figure pottery, Roman mosaics, and French Sèvres porcelain.

But while beautiful, her remixes of traditional ceramics are off-kilter vignettes of domesticity. She offers a conscious disconnect between objects and influences in large-scale three-dimensional collages. With an unapologetic riot of pattern and texture, she "Frankensteins" sculptures from commonplace objects, such as sneakers, laundry detergent, and garbage bags, which she camouflages with the ornamental language of elite decorative arts. Through this façade, she blurs the lines between high and low and craft and art, destabilizing hierarchies of value. Furthermore, DiMattio plays with material performativity through work where things are often not what they seem: clay can be fiber, and paint can be ceramic.

—AVL

Blue Wedgewood, 2023. Glaze on porcelain

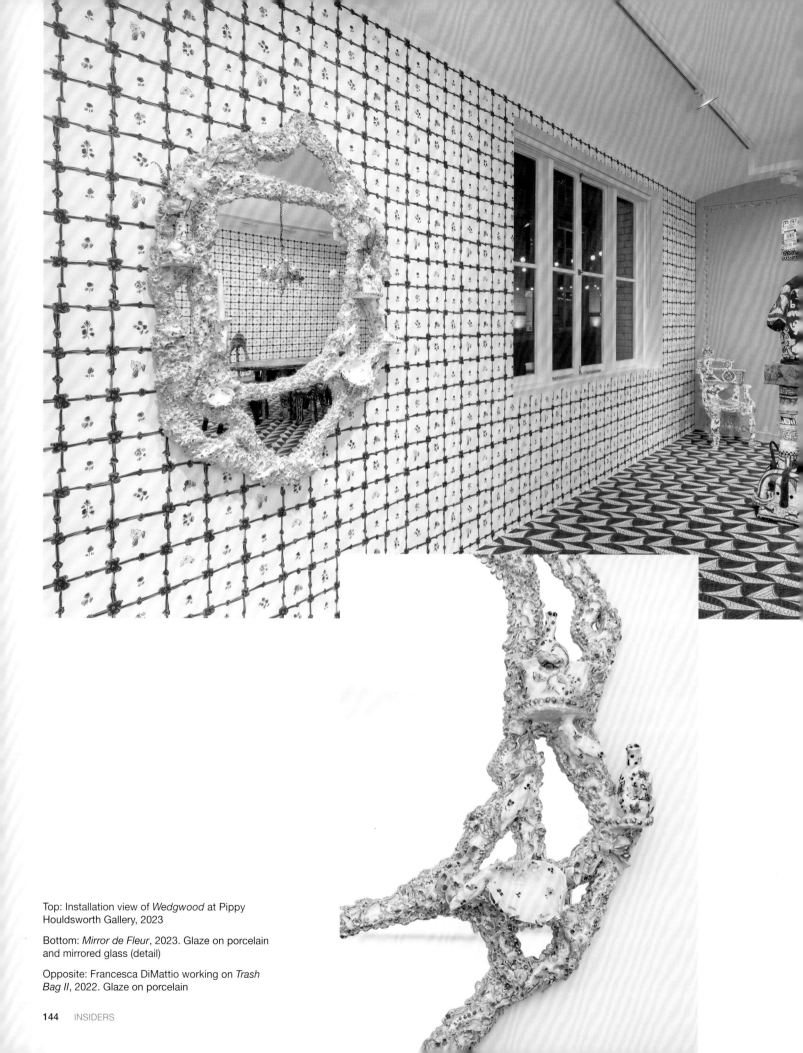

Top: Installation view of *Wedgwood* at Pippy
Houldsworth Gallery, 2023

Bottom: *Mirror de Fleur*, 2023. Glaze on porcelain
and mirrored glass (detail)

Opposite: Francesca DiMattio working on *Trash
Bag II*, 2022. Glaze on porcelain

Roxanne Jackson

B. Hayward, CA
Lives and works in Brooklyn, NY, and Wassaic, NY
roxannejackson.com
@roxannejackson_

Roxanne Jackson is dead serious about making fun work. From lustrous large-scale dragons that appear to weave in and out of the ground to beheaded animal cornucopias of guts and finger foods, her sculptures are a feast for the eyes that provoke a battle between attraction and repulsion. Delectable-looking cakes, tropical birds, tree stumps, witches' garments, and vases adorned with snakes or botanical specimens are just some of the other sculptural elements in her ceramic arsenal.

Jackson often stacks these items into topsy-turvy towers to perform a specific function: hold a single, spindly candlestick. The object's utility is almost an afterthought to the highly embellished sculptural body adorned with layers of extreme glaze, luster, and decals: a stepladder might be necessary to light the flame atop these absurd monoliths. Disinterested in what is comfortable or beautiful, Jackson subverts the expectations of utility and practicality for not only a candleholder but also other recognizable domestic components, such as vases and cake platters. Each of her pieces is a cabinet of curiosities of flora, fauna, and fantasy that rejects standards of domesticity and femininity.

—AVL

Opposite: *Crystal*, 2023. Ceramic, glaze, and luster

Snailz Vessel, 2021. Ceramic, glaze, and luster

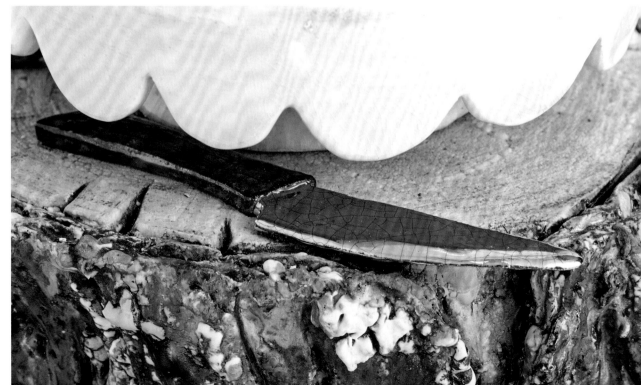

Tropical Goth Candle Holder, 2022. Ceramic, glaze, underglaze, luster, steel base, and epoxy

Katie Stout

B. 1989, Portland, ME
Lives and works in Germantown, NY
katiestout.com
@ummmsmile

Much has changed in Katie Stout's life in the past few years. She moved her studio out of Brooklyn, New York, to the Hudson Valley, where she lives and works in a nineteenth-century deconsecrated church, embracing a new form of domesticity and country life.

In a 2022 interview with the *New York Times*, Stout proclaimed that "walking the line between beauty and vulgarity feels so good."[1] Yet one could make the case that in her recent work, she has embraced sublimity over raunch. Witness her *Fruit Lady* floor lamp series, with bronze foliate armatures, ceramic gourds, and Victorian-style glass shades. Each fruit appears to be on the verge of overripe, in an exploration of how beauty and decay can coexist as rotting makes room for new growth. Or take, in another example, her monumental *Sphinx*, a sculpture that was situated in the grand hall of the Montreal Museum of Fine Arts, guarding the entrance to their 2023 exhibition *Parall(elles): A History of Women in Design*. Here the busty "girl" seen in her earlier works is transformed into an impressive winged lion inspired by the alabaster palace guards of the ancient city of Nimrud.

Stout's 2022 holiday windows for Hermès in New York are proof that she hasn't lost the ability to go over the top with festive kitsch. But her furniture and sculptures have become painterly and pastoral, reflecting both her new surroundings as well as her maturation as an artist.

—JZ

1 Katie Stout, in Noor Brara, "Artist and Furniture Designer Katie Stout Wandering Outside Her Studio," *T: The New York Times Style Magazine*, April 21, 2022, https://www.nytimes.com/2022/04/21/t-magazine/katie-stout.html.

Viola, 2023. Ceramic and luster

Opposite: *Vicky (The Joker)*, 2021. Ceramic, bronze, glass, and gold luster

Next pages: Katie Stout working on *Janet*, 2021

Bottom: Sketch for *Fruit Lady*, 2021

Right: *Sasha*, 2022. Ceramics, bronze, and glass

Collin Leitch

B. 1993, Mount Kisco, NY
Lives and works in Queens, NY
collinleitch.net
@collin.rn

Collin Leitch combines his experience as a filmmaker with his love for "thingness" to make "entertainment centers," a contemporary riff on a classic mainstay in American culture: the TV. Using a substantial collection of scanned film media, including negatives of photos and 16 mm and 35 mm film, Leitch amalgamates a diverse array of analog cinematic sources absent of fixed digital resolution to create video collages formatted for a 4K tilted screen. He doesn't take resolution for granted; rather, resolution becomes the subject of his pieces.

To house the videos, Leitch creates hybrid reinterpretations of vintage TV monitor housing that recall the cumbersome teak credenzas of the mid-century and the thick plastic frames in the early 2000s. The results are dimensional, ambiguous compositions. The rough layer lines that identify the 3D-printed PLA plastic are akin to the analog video scan lines and pixels present in the videos, which the artist appreciates; the marks show the physical limit to how much information can be kept in each type of output.

As Leitch observes, "The whole history of television as furniture and video art is so entwined."[1] Indeed, before "video art" had a name (and when separate playback devices didn't yet exist), video artists also called their works "television." The design polemic found in the furniture/sculpture tension, there from video's inception, remains a recurring theme in his work, as well as curious fodder in the art/design landscape of today.

—KR

---

1 Collin Leitch, interview by Kellie Riggs, July 17, 2023.

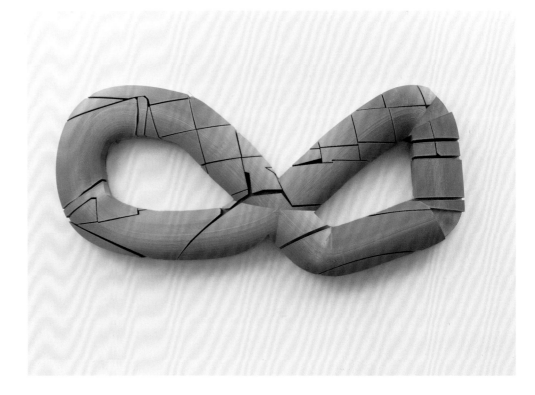

FS03, 2023. 3D-printed polylactic acid, medium density fiberboard, and spray paint

Opposite: *Vieiwing*, 2021. 4K video, monitor, media player, 3D-printed polylactic acid, walnut, and AV cables

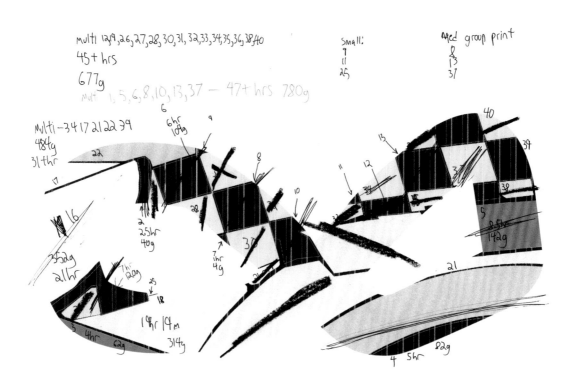

Top: Production sketch, 2023. Inkjet print, ballpoint pen, and china marker on paper

Bottom, left: Collin Leitch in his studio, 2023

Bottom, right, and opposite: *Endeavor*, 2019. 4K video, monitor, media player, 3D printed polylactic acid, wood, spray paint, stain, and AV cables

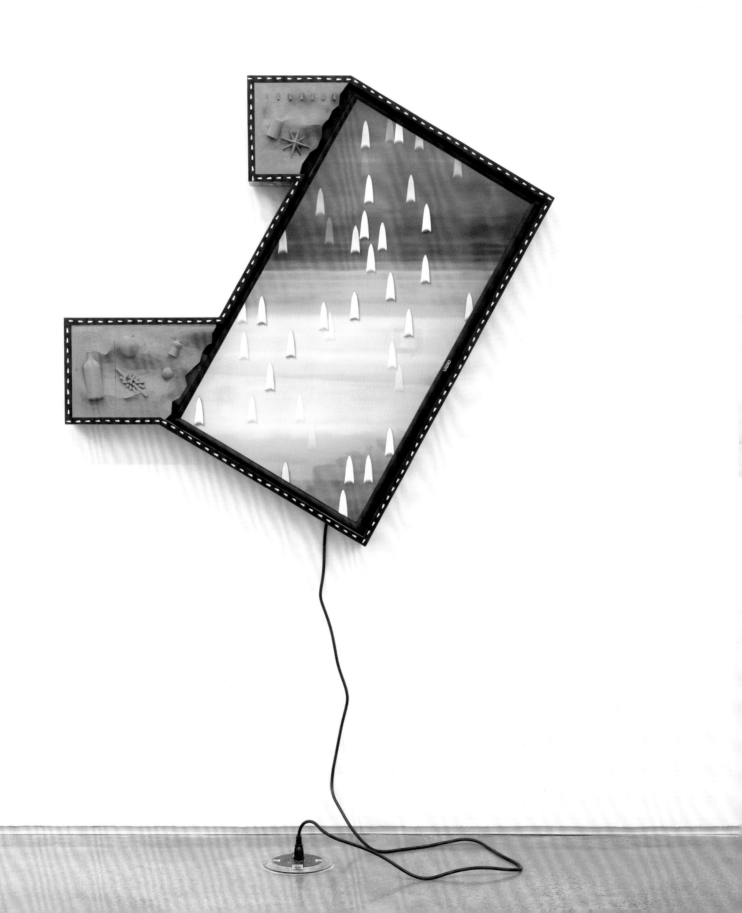

Anne Libby

B. 1987, Los Angeles, CA
Lives and works in Los Angeles, CA
@annelibby

The window has long been a foundational source of inspiration for sculptor Anne Libby, who appreciates its duality. Like a vessel, windows hold something in, but their transparency also allows for passage. She describes window blinds, the element used to both obscure and reveal what lies outside our domains, as an ephemeral gesture, or "barely an object,"[1] that she transfers into a static, opaque, distorted representation of itself in various materials like quilted textile, glass, and metal. Her *These Days* wall sculptures are dramatically long and appear caught in distorted movement. Their captured fleetingness creates surreal perspectives that aim to reflect on the more inward aspects of the human condition like loneliness, impermanence, and personal boundaries.

Alternatively in the round, Libby's *Inner Echo* pieces employ stacked louvered glass panes meant to open and close like jalousie windows but seemingly stuck halfway in between. A closer look reveals puddles of slumped glass on their steel structures, an exploration of the spectrum between transparent and opaque. From different vantage points the work invites a unique, disorienting experience of looking through multiple window-like planes at once; the effect evocative of infinity mirrors, which reflect yourself to the nth degree. In an age of endless gaze on social media and the blending of the public and the private, Libby's works are an astute reconceptualization of perception, privacy, and envy, concepts always fluctuating and relative to us all.

—KR

1 Anne Libby, interview by Kellie Riggs, October 5, 2023.

These Days, 240, 2022. Aluminum

Opposite: *Hourglass*, 2020. Satin, batting, and wood

Installation view of *Inner Green Echo* at Magenta
Plains, 2023

Opposite: *Half Past, 2:2,* 2022. Aluminum

Liam Lee

B. 1993, New York, NY
Lives and works in Brooklyn, NY
studioliamlee.com
@studio_liamlee

Liam Lee's felted furniture is a fantasy come to life. The architect of his dream world, Lee navigates the boundaries between interior and exterior spaces and the human-made and organic through domestic objects inspired by natural environments. Through a labor-intensive process, the self-taught artist builds armatures out of plywood, onto which he needle-felts hand-dyed merino wool to make chairs in radiating color gradients resembling coral and anemones. The smoothness of their bulbous and sinuous bodies blurs a point of origin in their creation, demonstrating Lee's interest in spontaneous generation. In this alchemical principle, living organisms are born from non-living materials. His large-scale monochromatic tapestries resemble the microscopic landscape of bacteria while pointing to Lee's pursuit of bringing nature indoors. While studying English literature and poetry, Lee developed a sensitivity for the layered meaning of objects and how they can establish spatial memory. He provokes the paradoxical feeling of simultaneous recognition and unfamiliarity through his objects. The biological forms of Lee's chairs paired with the wall hangings in hues so bright that they appear toxic make for beautiful yet alien objects within a domestic context.

—AVL

Chair 05, 2021. Merino wool and cedar; *Untitled Tapestry (Green)*, 2021. Merino wool and mohair

Opposite: *Chair 07*, 2022. Merino wool and cedar; *Untitled Tapestry (Pink)*, 2022. Merino wool and mohair

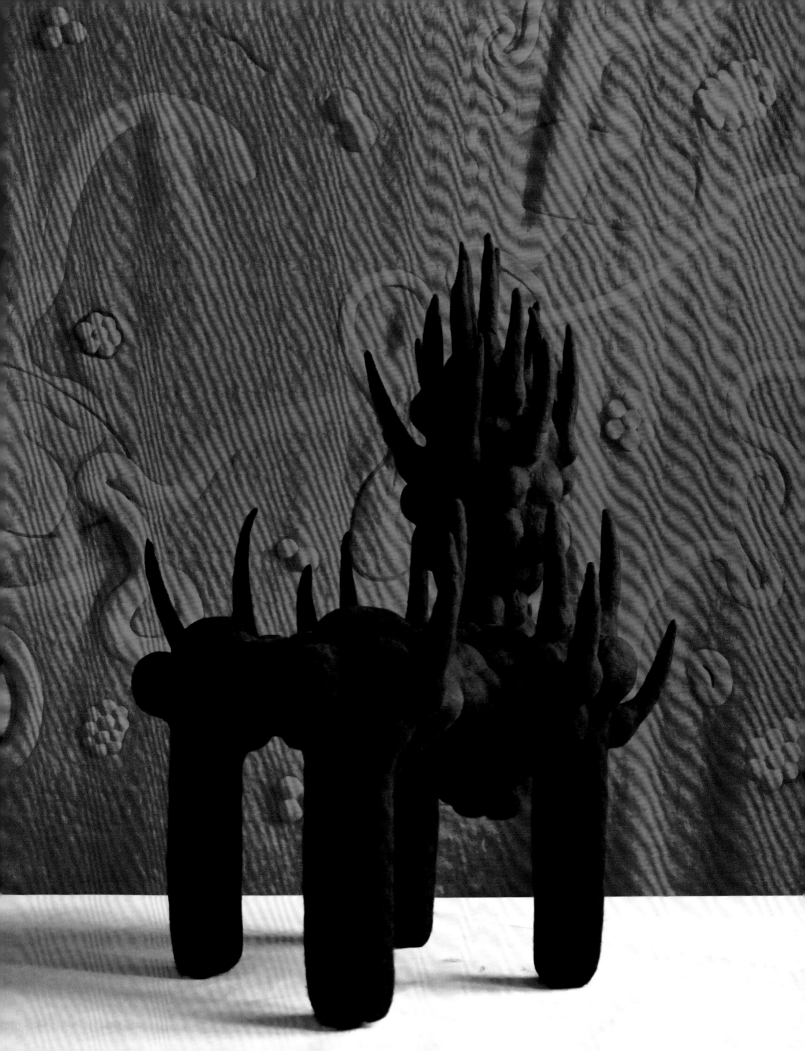

Chair 14, 2023. Merino wool and poplar plywood

Opposite, clockwise from top left: *Chair 04* (2021),
Chair 03 (2021), *Chair 01* (2021), *Chair 02* (2021).
Merino wool and cedar

Carl D'Alvia

B. 1965, Sleepy Hollow, NY
Lives and works in West Cornwall, CT
dalvia.com
@carldalvia

To say that Carl D'Alvia is a sculptor in the traditional sense is misleading, even though he is. Time-honored techniques and materials like lost-wax bronze casting have been a cornerstone of his practice, both detectable and admired. But his career has consistently subverted the more serious associations that come with those processes, like the purity of line, shape, and form, by creating rebellious figures. D'Alvia is known for employing humor and contradiction in his sculptures big or small, which activate any space they inhabit due to the conflicting energies that they give off: some slump and pout, or even smoke, while others look ready to throw shit around. The tension found in their hybrid nature, stuck somewhere between the stoic and the playful, is a continuing hallmark for D'Alvia, who has spent significant time in Italy. During his 2012 Rome Prize residency, he upset the perfectly manicured lawn of the American Academy with a giant cube bulging from under the grass.

He sees each piece he makes as a character—even his more recent works, which have entered the domain of "design." Familiar forms in his repertoire have gotten bigger, been upholstered and tufted, or been given wooden shingles fit for the roof of a house. Are they furniture, or sculptures of furniture? D'Alvia's response: "I'm trying to make the most figurative minimal sculpture, or the most minimal figurative sculpture . . . . If you buy it I cannot stop you from sitting on it."[1]

—KR

1 Carl D'Alvia, interview by Kellie Riggs, October 5, 2023.

Loveseat, 2021. Mixed media

Opposite: *Shroom Man*, 2022. Bronze

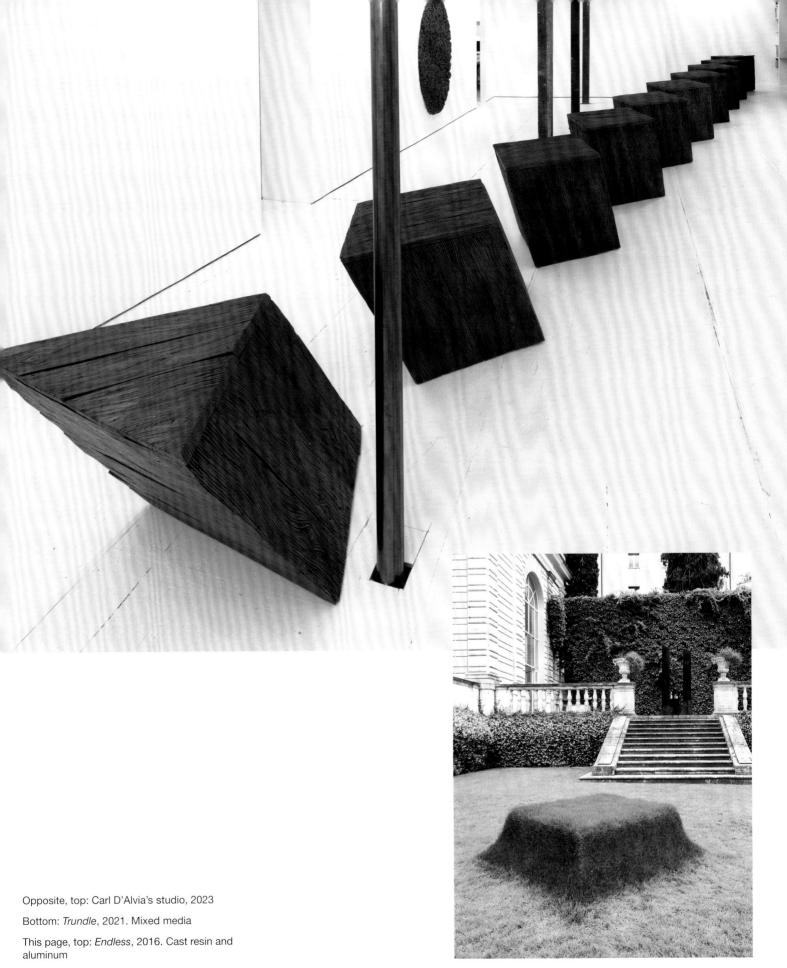

Opposite, top: Carl D'Alvia's studio, 2023

Bottom: *Trundle*, 2021. Mixed media

This page, top: *Endless*, 2016. Cast resin and aluminum

Bottom: *Visitor*, 2013. Grass and earth. Installation view at the American Academy in Rome, Italy

Linda Nguyen Lopez

B. 1981, Visalia, CA
Lives and works in Fayetteville, AR
lindalopez.net
@linda_lopez

Linda Nguyen Lopez's sculptural lamps double as furniture, inviting us to sit under the warm glow of a hand-blown lightbulb to rest, meditate, and dream. These pieces represent a marked departure in scale and function for the artist from the tabletop objects she is best known for—lumpy and furry sculptures inspired by making friends with dust bunnies and other household items as a child growing up in an immigrant home without a shared language. Her mother's anthropomorphization of the domestic realm left a lasting impact on how Lopez approaches object-making. The lamps symbolize a respite for the artist's complex emotions over a lifetime of making sense of her mixed identity while continuing her playful pursuit of animating the inanimate with a touch of humor. The two-in-one sculptures' cloud-like appearance and exposed wiring running upwards make for an illusion of airiness—as if they could float away—that belies their sturdy composition. She adorns their amorphous bodies through a labor-intensive process of hand-cutting tiles into shapes found in textiles from her Vietnamese and Mexican heritage and puzzling them into sparkling, ombré candy-colored formations.

—AVL

Dust Furries, 2022. Porcelain

Opposite: *Floating Ground*, 2021. Ceramic, epoxy, grout, tala bulb, and lamp hardware

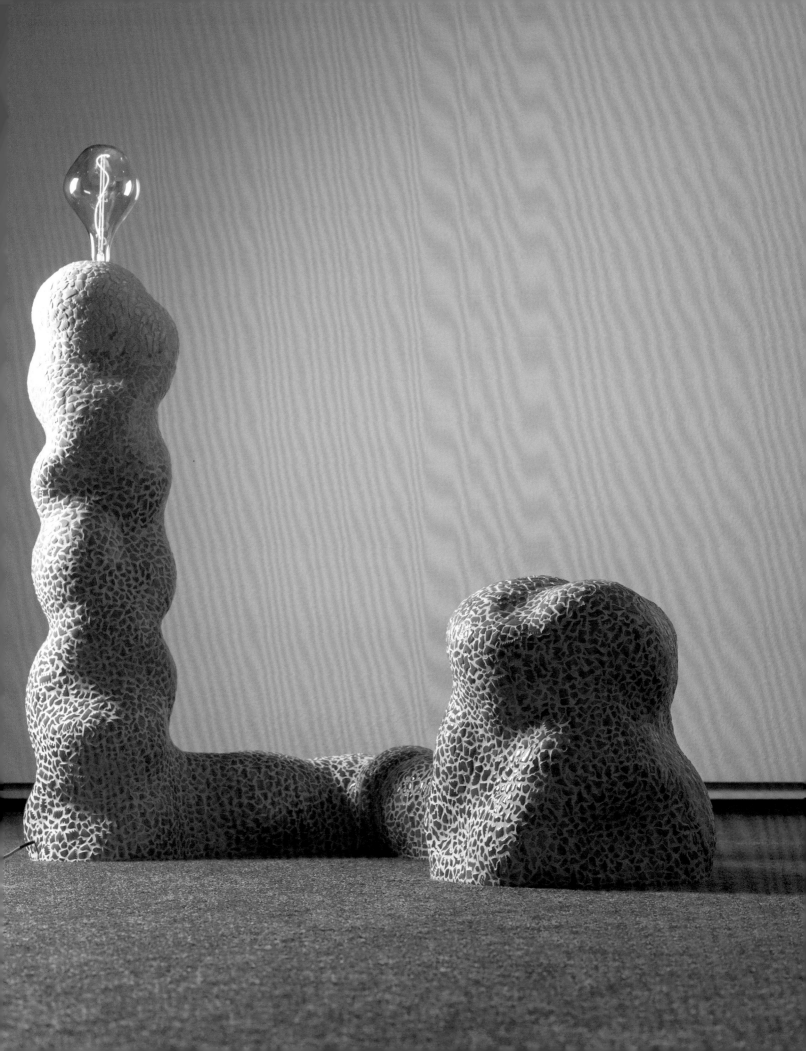

Clockwise from top left: *I Know a Place*, 2023. Porcelain, earthenware, and grout; detail of *Floating Ground*; loose mosaic tiles in Linda Nguyen Lopez's studio, 2023

Opposite: *Long Lost*, 2021. Ceramic, epoxy, grout, tala bulb, and lamp hardware

Hugh Hayden

B. 1983, Dallas, TX
Lives and works in New York City, NY
hughhayden.com
@huthhayden

Depending on your point of entry, Hugh Hayden's distortion of quotidian household items might hit differently. Do they feel bizarre? Like fun? Failure? There are no wrong answers. Relative concepts like success, achievement, assimilation, and struggle are all at play in his sometimes massive, other times tender artworks and installations. Hayden makes critical objects. Taken-for-granted everyday things like cribs, dining tables, and hairbrushes contradict themselves with strange but familiar interventions, obtrusive appendages, or oppositional materials for the implied function. From their standpoint, they are perceptive criticisms, observant but nuanced reflections of the disillusionment of our country's self-proclaimed promise for an abundant and secure future for all. Hayden's work embodies a different reality, one that knows this is true for only some.

The relational quality of his work has been a constant in his practice. With a love for cooking, Hayden's past culinary installations have undoubtedly influenced the surreal mise-en-scènes he now creates, filled with subverted objects, animated kitchenware, and challenging furnishings that require cooperation and consideration. In a way, they are solution-oriented; by turning what might go invisible to some into something glaring, Hayden's practice emphasizes his desire to generate structural change for others like him in the real world. In 2021, he formed the Solomon B. Hayden Fellowship to provide financial support and art world mentorship opportunities for deserving students demonstrating leadership in African American and African Diaspora communities.

—KR

Start 'Em Young, 2023. Chain link fencing and hardware

Opposite: *Huey*, 2021. Rattan and plywood

Next pages: *America*, 2018. Mesquite and plywood

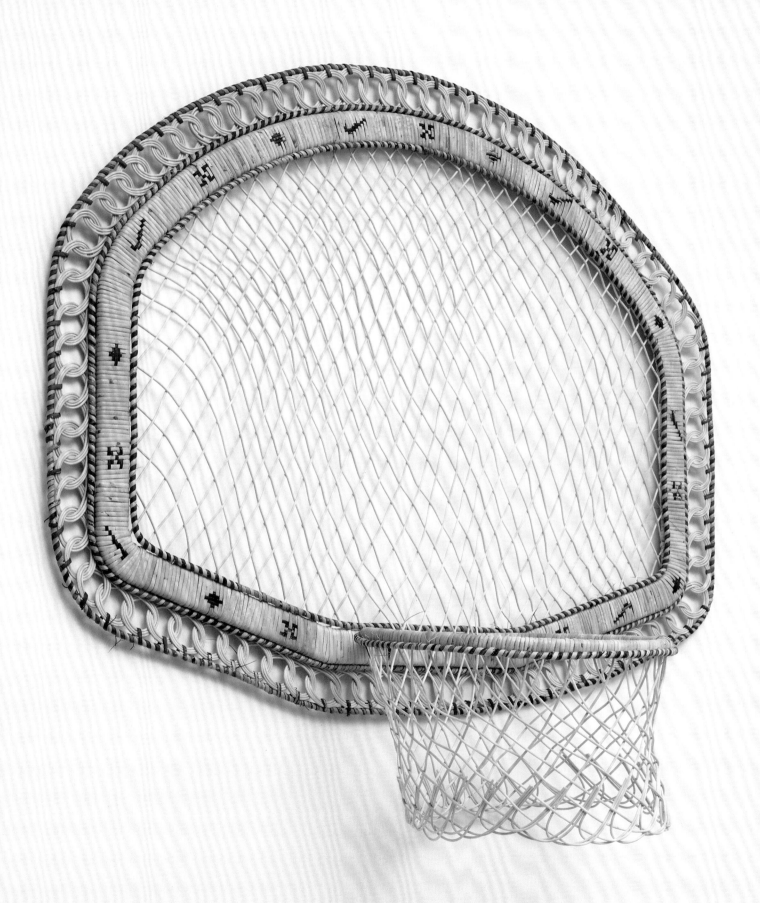

Nicki Green

B. 1986, Boston, MA
Lives and works in Alfred, NY
nickigreen.org
@nickigreenstudio

Nicki Green reconceptualizes the bathroom and the ceramic objects within it as sacred liminal spaces for transformation. She breaks down the expected utility of commonplace domestic objects through hybrids of toilet tanks, sinks, bidets, urinals, and faucets holding lavender sprigs like Dutch tulip vases to make memorials of change. In reference to the grandeur of liturgical objects, Green adorns her work with illustrations of moons, mushrooms, water, and other symbols of transformation as reminders that change is an intrinsic part of living.

Her large ceramic bathtubs are symbolic containers for the care of people through the ritual of bathing. This body of work is a nod to her Jewish heritage and the mikvah, traditionally a ceremonial bath for women after menstruation or birth that has evolved to be a more inclusive practice of healing, creativity, and commemoration of significant life changes. Her interventions into delftware, where earthenware pretends to be porcelain, underscore ideas of conceptual and political performativity, especially as she creates what she refers to as a "failure of illusion" by allowing the clay body to peek through the glaze. Furthermore, she subverts the traditional blue-and-white palette with lavender, a symbol of resistance for the LGBTQ+ community.

—AVL

Splitting/Unifying (toilet tanks, slip spigots and medical sink laver with faucets), 2019. Glazed vitreous china, epoxy, and found slip spigots

Opposite: *The Porous Sea (Tank)*, 2019. Glazed earthenware, cotton quilt, walnut, and caning

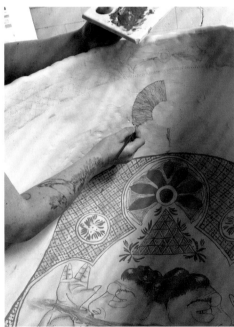

Clockwise from top left: Detail of *Splitting/ Unifying*; *The Porous Sea (Tub)*, 2019. Glazed earthenware and cotton quilt (top and side views); Nicki Green working on *The Porous Sea*

Opposite: *Hybrid Vessel 1*, 2020. Glazed earthenware

Wally Dion

B. 1976, Saskatoon, Canada
Lives and works in Binghamton, NY
wallydion.com
@wally_dion

For many years, Wally Dion has been working with a venerated and cherished symbol to North American Indigenous people: the eight-pointed star, or Morning Star. Its precise origin story and what it represents varies from tribe to tribe. But across Native Nations, it commonly appears on regalia, beadwork, and blankets, which are gifted at celebratory rites of passage for either the giver or the receiver. Dion, who is Yellow Quill First Nation, has become an unconventional quilter of star blankets. The fascination began before he knew how to sew, his first "quilts" being made of circuit board pieces that spoke about environmental waste and Indigenous activism.

A decade and a half later, Dion is skillfully equipped with a needle and thread, electing for translucent, monochromatic material with which to sew the motif into giant flags. His four *Prairie Tall Grass Quilts*, named *Bison*, *Fire*, *Grass*, and *Winter*, exist to represent the native ecosystems that flourished in the Great Plains region before the arrival of settlers. Whether shown on their own or superimposed onto one another, the flags are stunning. He says, "I understand that I am working in an area, geographically as well as emotionally, where people feel a great sense of denial and dissonance towards their colonial histories. I sometimes feel that there is a lot of weight in these topics and it would be nice to have a place of visual relaxation and calm."[1]

—KR

1 Wally Dion, interview by Kellie Riggs, September 29, 2023.

Evening Star, Morning Star, 2019. Circuit boards, auto paint, steel wire, and steel tube

Opposite: *Grass Quilt*, 2022. Various fabrics

Prairie Tall Grass Quilts, 2023. Fabric and
copper pipe

Opposite: *Bison Quilt*, 2023. Fabric and
copper pipe

Jason McDonald

B. 1984, Tacoma, WA
Lives and works in Tacoma, WA
jasonmcdonaldglass.com
@jasonmcdonald42

Jason McDonald's contemporary glass practice explores the boundaries imposed by the material, his skills, and society. With a passion for sixteenth-century Venetian furnace techniques, such as stem-working and caneworking, he meticulously crafts elegant goblets and chalices in a virtuosic pursuit. However, he also makes sculptures to reflect on his lived experience as a Black man in the United States. As an artist and educator, he advocates for making the field of studio glass, which has historically been dominated by white artists, more accessible to diverse communities. He travels nationally to do workshops and was a contestant on the second season of Netflix's competition series *Blown Away*.

Through his practice, McDonald is doing away with gatekeeping. His work is purposely ornamental to lure people in for a closer look. His large-scale ironwork gates, adorned with delicate flourishes of transparent and white glass canes, break the illusion of protection. Instead, they underscore the fragility and futility of traditional structures and systems that deny access to specific groups of people. These objects symbolize McDonald taking control over his destiny as a maker while opening the door for others to work with glass.

—AVL

Gatekeeper, 2023. Glass, found object, steel, glue, and paint

Opposite: *A Self-Made Trap*, 2022. Glass and wood

Left: *Medusa Cup*, 2022. Glass

Right: *Besieged*, 2019. Glass (detail)

Opposite: *Gatekeeper* (detail)

Norman Teague

B. 1968, Chicago, IL
Lives and works in Chicago, IL
normanteaguedesignstudios.com
@normanteaguedesignstudios

"I don't feel like I'm doing a good job unless somebody's picking up part of what I am putting down."[1] Norman Teague's response to a question by Glenn Adamson in *Smithsonian Magazine* reflects his emphasis on teaching and collaboration. Teague's lodestar is in the neighborhood of South Chicago, where he designs furniture and interiors for locally owned businesses and uses his socially engaged practice to collaborate with the community.

Teague is best known in the museum world for his rocking chair designs, a quintessentially American form that has been underexplored since the prime years of Sam Maloof. Drawing on a host of inspirations ranging from vernacular examples seen on the front porches of Black and Brown Chicagoans to African traditional techniques in carving and leatherwork, Teague designed two consecutive

masterworks: The *Sinmi Stool*—a radical and sexy new chapter in the modernist bentwood canon—and the *Africana Rocking Chair*, which is rootsier and more suited for the stoop.

In addition to managing his studio and teaching at the University of Illinois, Chicago, Teague has turned his attention to recycling and weaving extruded plastics into vessel forms, which were included in *Everlasting Plastics*, a poignant exhibition at the U.S. Pavilion for the 2023 Venice Architecture Biennale. Teague continues to spin new works out of discarded plastic containers for milk and laundry detergent once a week at a local factory.

—JZ

1 Glenn Adamson, "The State of American Craft Has Never Been Stronger," *Smithsonian Magazine*, January 2021, https://www.smithsonianmag.com/arts-culture/state-american-craft-never-been-stronger-180976483/.

Right and opposite, top: *Diasporic Mural*, 2022. Plywood, cushion, and fabric

Opposite, bottom: *Sinmi Stool*, 2020. Birch plywood, Baltic birch legs, pony skin, and leather

Africana Chair and *Africana Rocking Chair*, 2020.
Basswood and leather

Opposite: *Extruded Vessel #16,* 2023. Plastic

Justin Favela

B. 1986, Las Vegas, NV
Lives and works in Las Vegas, NV
@favyfav

In his practice, Justin Favela reclaims the piñata as a symbol of Latine identity while spoofing the art historical canon that has prioritized white artists for centuries. The festive visual language of the piñata spreads onto unexpected objects and across walls to create immersive installations that celebrate Chicano culture and Favela's Central American heritage. His fringed works range in scale from still-life paintings to life-size lowriders. Favela's tapestries and site-specific installations are colorful, sweeping landscapes at a distance but become distorted and abstracted upon closer inspection, drawing attention to their piñata-like composition.

The iconic party decoration, often shaped like popular figures in television and other media, also serves as an archive of what is popular. With his chosen subject matter, Favela expands the concept of American pop culture beyond the borders of the United States and establishes a dialogue between the lowbrow and highbrow. Traditional piñatas become more valuable once the rewards they hold inside spill, yet despite Favela using the same cheap and accessible materials as the traditional versions—cardboard and tissue paper—the context and scale of Favela's work are impossible to ignore, provoking consideration of their imagery and its cultural significance.

—AVL

Piñata Motel, 2016. Paper and glue on existing motel

Opposite: *Cardón, after José María Velasco*, 2018. Tissue paper and glue on board

Next pages: *Recuérdame*, 2018. Paper and glue on wall, installation at Sugar Hill Children's Museum of Art and Storytelling

Dee Clements

B. 1980, Rochester, NY
Lives and works in Chicago, IL
studioherron.com
@studio_herron

The founder and director of Studio Herron, Dee Clements, is not one to shy away from the craft roots that inform her design practice. The avid researcher has traveled the world learning about the ethnography of objects and craft disciplines through a feminist lens, ultimately leading her to basketry. Although guided by a deep appreciation for materials and respect for traditional methodologies, especially those historically stewarded by women, the designer wants basket weaving to run wild.

She zigzags between tight and loose weaves, often intentionally leaving the structures unfinished to create abstract sculptural forms at a grand scale. Painterly surfaces built through multicolor hand-dyed reeds and gouache heighten the freedom of form. Despite their undeniable basket quality, they are not containers but voluptuous and expressive objects that intervene with space to investigate the relationship between bodies and social space. Clements's creations look and behave like human bodies: lumpy, bumpy, and sometimes droopy or on the verge of collapse. Specifically, they reference the bodies and experiences of women. The anthropomorphic baskets are rebellious proxies for one of the most significant legacies of women's work.

—AVL

Largesse with Frills, 2023–24. Ceramic, reed, dye, paint, and polyurethane

Opposite: *Woman Seated*, 2023. Reed, dye, gouache paint, spray paint, ceramic, and polyurethane

Left: *Lilith*, 2023. Reed, dye, gouache paint, spray paint, and polyurethane (detail)

Right: *Things to Lean On*, 2023–24. Ceramic, reed, dye, milk paint, wood, and spray paint

Opposite, top: Installation view of *The Future has an Ancient Heart* at Nina Johnson Gallery, 2023

Bottom: Dee Clements in her studio, 2023

Luam Melake

B. 1986, San Diego, CA
Lives and works in New York, NY
luammelake.com

"America has an alienation problem from which many other societal ills spring,"[1] says Luam Melake, who believes that the social media of the digital age are destructive forces. Divergently, she creates furniture that encourages personal and emotional engagement, transforming ordinary interactions into intimate moments. The various positions one can take on her pieces—inclined or upright, relaxed or attentive—suggest active or passive stances, and these variations allow users to favor or evade eye contact, engage in casual chats or emotional discussions, meditate or confess. The resulting dynamics, capable of "furnishing feelings" (the title of her 2023 solo exhibition at R & Company), promote new ways of connecting with others.

When it comes to materials, Melake is no Luddite. Her signature urethane and polyurethane foam technique is inspired by the experiments of late 1960s Italian Radicals, but updated to reflect twenty-first-century concerns about sustainability, which she has explored in her position as director of research at the Healthy Materials Lab at Parsons School of Design. Melake's most recent design, the *Barber Chair* for the *Black in Design* collection by CB2, is inspired by the vinyl seating of Harlem barber shops, with additional historicism gleaned from French tubular steel designs of the 1920s. Melake writes, "The chair itself is a stand-in for an entire community—a social space and a ritual that's a part of the Black experience."[2]

—JZ

1 Luam Melake, in The Editors, "The 2022 American Design Hot List, Part IV," Sight Unseen, January 26, 2023, https://www.sightunseen.com/2023/01/the-2022-american-design-hot-list-part-iv/.
2 Luam Melake, "Special Projects," Luam Melake, accessed November 14, 2023, https://www.luammelake.com/projects.

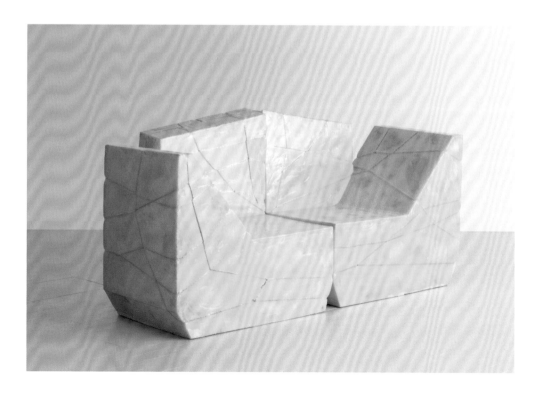

Love Seat in Two Parts, 2022. Urethane, polyurethane foam, dyes, and jute twine

Opposite: *Unwinding Chair*, 2022. Urethane, polyurethane foam, and dyes

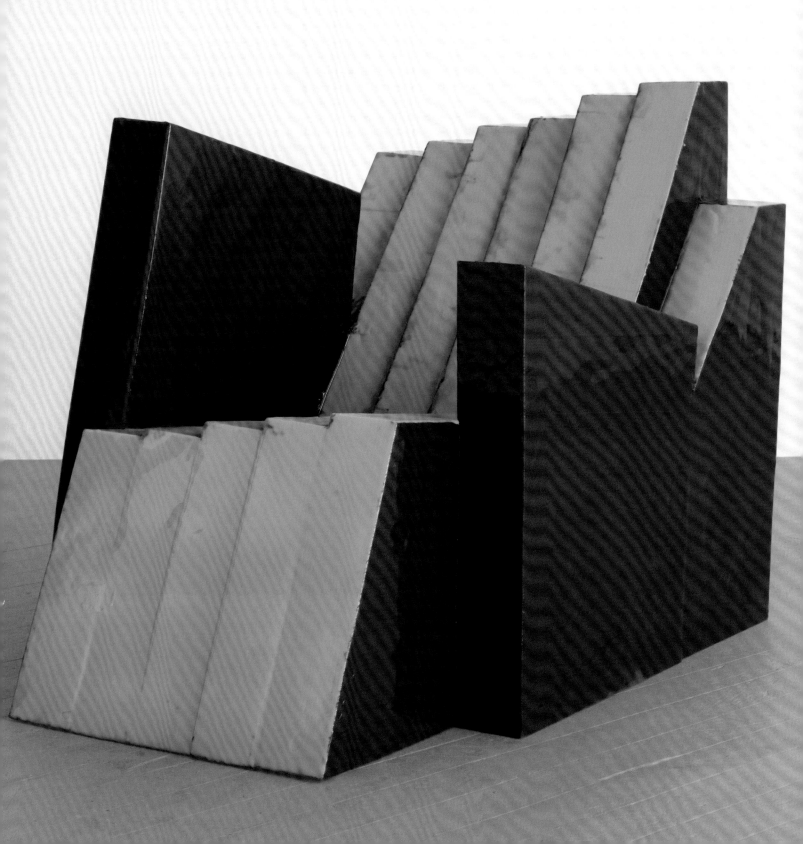

The *Love Seat in Two Parts* in its various
configurations

Opposite: *Occasional Table, Bench, Chair*, 2021.
Urethane, plywood, polyurethane foam, and dyes;
Regressive Chair, 2022. Urethane, polyurethane
foam, and dyes

Misha Kahn

B. 1989, Duluth, MN
Lives and works in Brooklyn, NY
mishakahn.com
@mishakahn

Misha Kahn is a polymath who aspires to differentiate the concept of "process" from that of "building." He says that the former can be anything, and it often does not relate to the construction of our physical realm, only the visual. In his eyes, building is largely taken for granted, only an irrelevant means to an end with arbitrary meaning. He describes it as a void. What does it then mean to build in a different way? What happens when making something is no longer inextricable from efficiency or visual language? It is not surprising that the son of a house builder and children's book author would question his trade in this way, especially against the backdrop of the imaginative, transfigurative material remarkability that has defined his career.

However, Kahn has always loved the perfect attachment that combines one element of a work with another to enclose something just right, to use structure as form inventively. Going forward, he wants to answer the call of whether or not building something, at every step, could respond in reverie to our sense of being, the earth, our emotions, and the metaphysical. It is his rebuttal to the pressure of constantly having to innovate, to the criticism of using too many materials or using them in the wrong way. He says, "I want to make a language, a rich lexicon of methods that together fabricate a holistic landscape of the material world that is deeply human."[1]

—KR

1 Misha Kahn, interview by Kellie Riggs, October 10, 2023.

Mole Eats Worm, 2020. Foam, fabric, and steel (full view and detail on next pages)

Opposite: *For Those Who Float*, 2022. Plastic and paint (side and bottom views)

Cedric Mitchell

B. 1986, Tulsa, OK
Lives and works in Los Angeles, CA
cedricmitchelldesign.com
@cedricmitchelldesign

A musician who fell in love with studio glass, Cedric Mitchell is no stranger to sampling a wide range of influences in his practice. His *Modern Funk* series combines the bold attitude and eclectic style of 1970s and '80s funk music, the playfulness of Memphis Milano furniture, the aesthetics of 1990s toys and street art, and the minimalism of modern design into one-of-a-kind sculptures and vases. He forges each geometric component with precision and dedication in a saturated candy-colored palette. Mitchell then mixes and matches the pieces into stacking whimsical tabletop sculptures. He also makes functional wares that similarly engage color and shapes.

Mitchell navigates his growing career while developing a social practice as an organizer and educator with dexterity. For the past ten years, he has actively supported emerging artists and disseminated knowledge about making glass art through his involvement with youth organizations in underserved communities that have historically not had access to art education. He is also on the leadership team of Crafting the Future, an artist-run organization that provides scholarships for young artists of color to connect with craft-based educational opportunities. Mitchell is looking to shatter the glass ceiling of the art world for generations to come.

—AVL

Works from *The Object Lounge* collection for Heath Ceramics, 2023

Opposite: *Static Motion*, 2023. Glass

Cedric Mitchell in the hot shop, 2023

Opposite: *Lurid*, 2023. Glass (detail)

Trey Jones

B. 1984, Lexington, KY
Lives and works in Washington, DC
treyjonesstudio.com
@treyjones_studio

A decade into his career, Trey Jones looked to define his point of view through sculptural furniture. His "aha!" moment came when he decided to reduce waste in his practice by addressing the overwhelming amount of plywood scraps in his studio. Based on the Japanese tradition of *nerikomi*—the stacking of colored porcelain to make canes that, when sliced through, reveal a pattern—he developed his signature "wood *nerikomi*." With this modified stacked lamination technique, Jones embraces the inherent qualities of salvaged plywood, breaking free from his minimalist modernist furniture design training to create complex and dynamic veneers for his sculptural furniture.

Jones's process is technically comparable to Wendell Castle's "stack lamination." However, unlike Castle's work, whose seamless surfaces deliberately obscure the clever and resourceful lamination technique, Jones celebrates the wild patterns found within the stacks. Adept at playing with color, he combines the regularity of patterns with organic sculptural forms to balance creative expression and utility. He not only puzzles together the surfaces of his furniture but designs modular components that allow for interaction, movement, and the reconfiguration of pieces to provide different functions and sculptural compositions.

—AVL

Trellis Chair, 2023. Reclaimed plywood, ash wood, dyes, and sealer

Opposite: *The River*, 2022. Reclaimed plywood, steel, brass, glass, dyes, and sealer

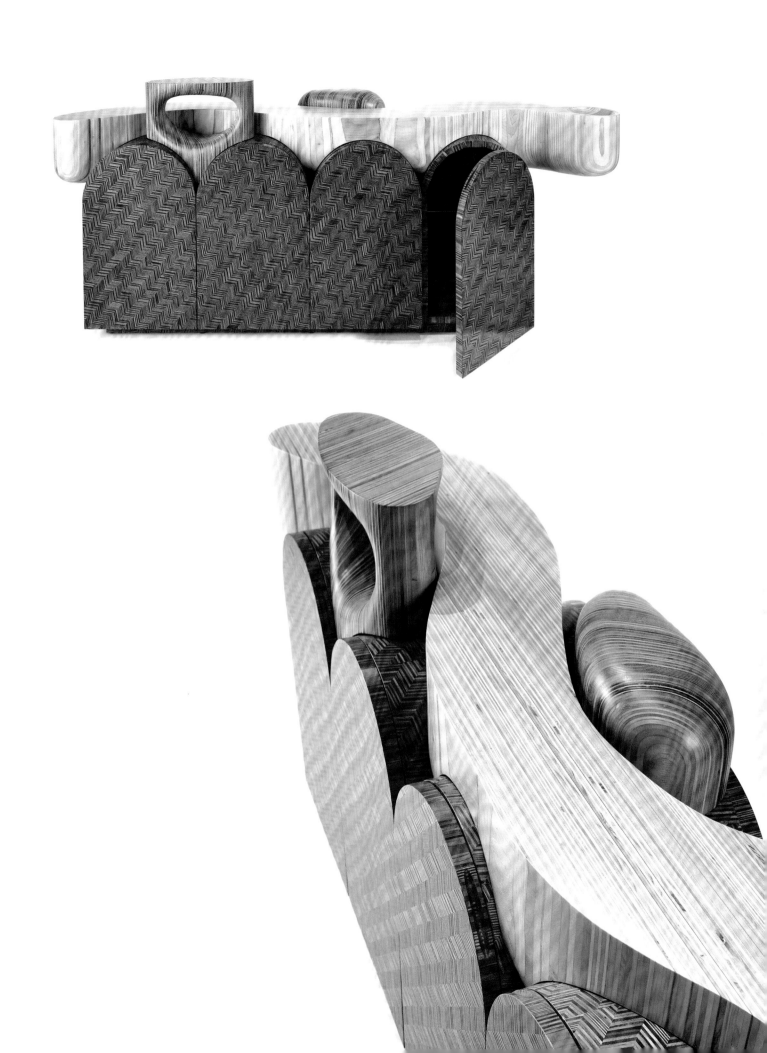

Plywood scraps and *nerikomi* samples in Trey Jones's studio, 2023

Opposite: *The Forest*, 2022. Reclaimed plywood, ash wood, brass, acrylic, glass, dyes, and sealer

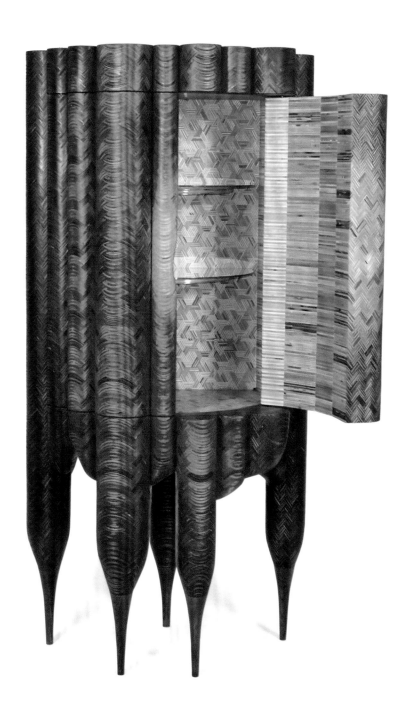

Richard Chavez

B. 1949, San Felipe Pueblo, NM
Lives and works in San Felipe Pueblo, NM
chavezstudio.com
@chavezstudio

The jewelry made by Richard Chavez stands apart from his Southwestern contemporaries because they are sleek, streamlined, and strikingly modern. The marriage of stone and metal is highly valued in the adornment traditions of the Zuni and other Pueblo tribes, Hopi, and Navajo, yet for over forty years, Chavez has looked beyond his region to find inspiration from other sources, like in the geometric simplicities of Bauhaus art. His background in architecture is also on full display in his pieces, for he is an excellent planner and draftsman. Continually inspired by architectural motifs found in buildings, he reinterprets intriguing angles or ratios of scale into rings, bolos, and more.

Chavez is a master in lapidary art and inlay—the process of taking chunks of raw stone and minerals and grinding them down to smaller parts so that they fit together perfectly and create harmonious designs. His dynamic compositions break planes in unexpected ways for his format, and at times seem to conceal the meticulous manual precision that each of their separate elements requires: in many of his black stone cuffs, the highly polished surface leaves almost no trace of its intricate modular construction. With no assistants, it is important to the jeweler to do every step himself. His unique repertoire also favors more unexpected material choices like black and green jade, beyond the turquoise and coral that have defined the tradition that Chavez has contemporized.

—KR

Brooch/Pin, 2000. Edwards black jade, coral, turquoise, dolomite, and 14-karat gold

Opposite: Several rings and a cuff in lapis lazuli, coral, turquoise, sterling silver, and 14-karat gold, 1990s

Left: Richard Chavez in his studio, 2020s

Bottom: *Ring*, 2000. Siberian green jade, coral, and 14-karat gold

Opposite: Several rings in lapis lazuli, coral, turquoise, sterling silver, and 14-karat gold, 1990s

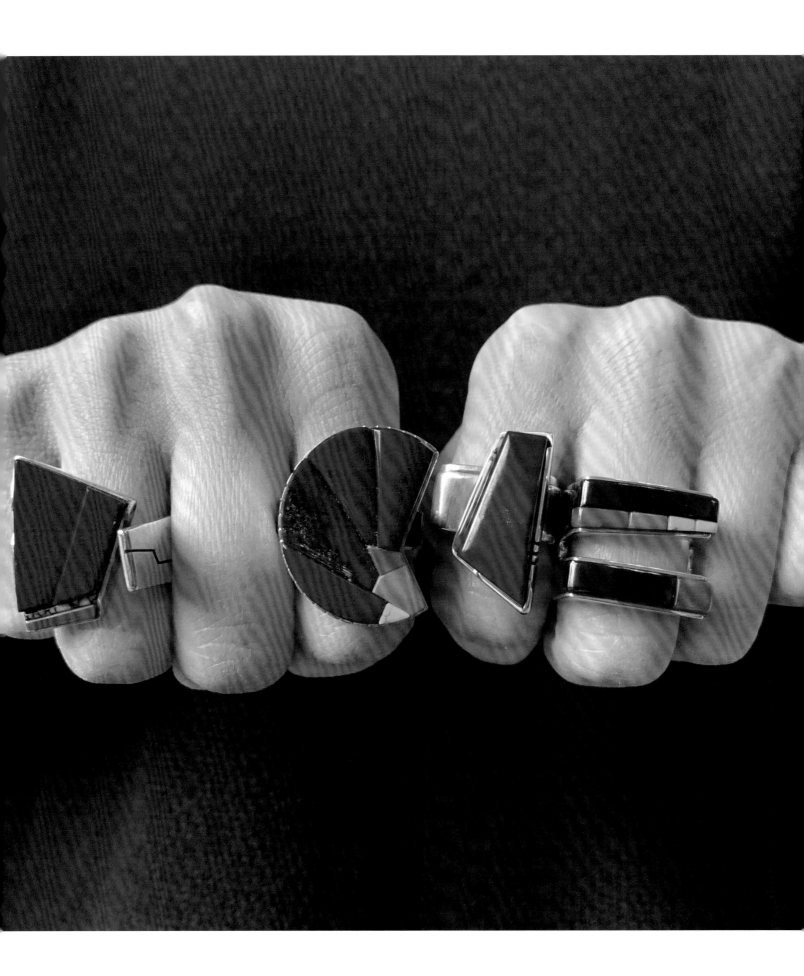

Kim Mupangilaï

B. 1989, Antwerp, Belgium
Lives and works in Brooklyn, NY
@pangilai

Furniture designer Kim Mupangilaï wants to believe in what she makes, creating a body of work filled with personal narrative and supporting evidence. Her collection *Kasai* is an exploration of self-identity, interpreted through a semi-coded material language. The allegiance to teak, stone, rattan, and banana fiber is symbolic to that of her Congolese heritage on her father's side. In the Congo, banana leaves are primarily used to wrap, cook, and store food. The designer got to know this material and stretched its functionality, drying the fiber for lampshades or to wrap around bench seats. By focusing on what becomes familiar, she can use it as her red thread to connect the dots of her story, which also comes from her Belgian mother and having been raised in Europe.

The shapes and details of the interlocking elements that compose her furniture are derived from currency tools common in all regions of pre-colonial Africa, where household items, knives, and jewelry used for bartering and commemorating births or marriages were often sculptural and decorated with engravings. Mupangilaï studied these objects, and sketched and abstracted their forms to create a personal alphabet. Her pieces thus require closer looking to reveal their complexities, including the subtle, extra functionalities they come with: a blanket hanging rack under the "armpit" of an armoire, or a small inset stone dish on the top of a side table. To live with Mupangilaï's work means to feel their generosity.

—KR

Bina Daybed, 2023. Teak, volcanic stone, and raffia

Opposite: *Brazza Screen*, 2023. Teak, volcanic stone, and rattan

Installation view of *Hue I Am / Hue Am I* at Superhouse, 2022

Opposite, clockwise from top left: *Bina Chair*, 2023. Teak, volcanic stone, and raffia (detail); *Bina Table*, 2023. Teak, volcanic stone, and rattan; *Bina Chair*; *Mwasi Armoire*, 2023. Teak, volcanic stone, and rattan (detail)

Steven KP

B. 1995, Milwaukee, WI
Lives and works in Providence, RI
stevenkp.com
@stevenkp_

Steven KP treats wood as an archive that acknowledges the past but never truly lets it go. The knot is a recurring symbol for the jeweler, who carves them to appear as though they are stuck in a similar liminal phase. It is also through making, slow and full of care, that KP attempts to find solace. Concepts like healing and passing have been important to the artist; the format of jewelry as a social signifier presents itself as the perfect conduit. Their work reflects on tending to something ending and allowing something new to be nurtured.

More recently, the jeweler has been thinking about the notion of clear-cutting, where saplings become vulnerable to threats when old-growth forests are cut down. As a queer person and the grandchild of a German Jewish cabinetmaker, this type of loss and erasure is familiar. When there is a lack of elders (and the safe places they maintain), there is a lack of guidance and protection and an inability for generational knowledge to transfer. By working in a familial language, KP's pieces reflect embodied wisdom that is able to connect, bind, and even replace heirlooms that have been lost. When things are torn down, new pathways need to be created; in carving, the artist seeks to follow the lines in wood grain akin to clearing a trail, and the objects act as flagging symbols so that anyone can find their way.

—KR

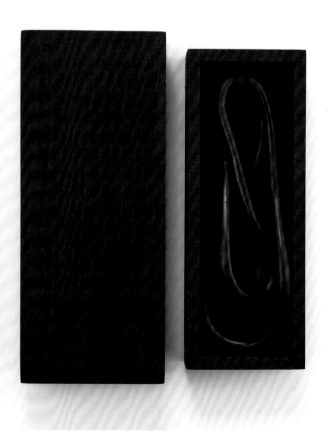

Double Over Pendant I, 2022. Cherry wood, sterling silver, and deerskin leather

Opposite: *Relief I*, 2022. Cherry wood, sterling silver, and lambskin

Steven KP in the studio, 2023

Opposite, clockwise from top left: *Madeira/
Timber*, 2023. Mahogany and sterling silver;
Partially Undone Knot, 2020. Cherry wood and
oxidized copper; *Partially Undone Knot (Medal)*,
2022. Cherry wood, sterling silver, and deerskin
leather

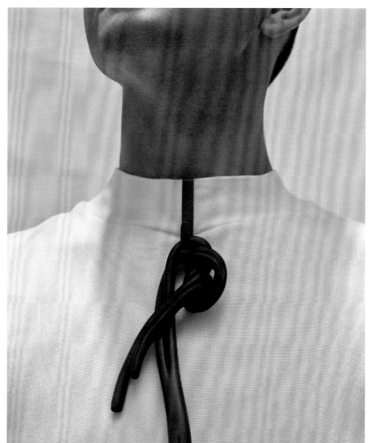

Jordan Nassar

B. 1985, New York, NY
Lives and works in Brooklyn, NY
jordannassar.com
@jordannassar

Jordan Nassar engages various mediums, including fiber, wood, and glass, in honoring his Palestinian heritage through the development of an imaginary utopia for diasporic identity. Although he was born and raised in New York, his nostalgia for a return to an ancestral home propels him to revisit serene scenes of rolling hills in the many formats of his practice. Best known for his embroidered canvases drawing from traditional Palestinian textile motifs, Nassar has collaborated with women weavers from the West Bank to create some of these works. The women choose the colors and stitches that serve as framing devices for open spaces that Nassar later fills with his archetypical landscape.

In a recent pursuit, Nassar began producing inlays of wood, mother-of-pearl, and brass that continue this exploration, using varying tones and grains that solidify the pixelation of his utopic visions. The material choices for his abstract, wavy mountains recall organic elements found within a natural environment. In the form of a bench, the landscape provides a symbolic place of rest and respite for displaced people. Nassar's work is hopeful yet conscious of the political realities that keep his world-building within the confines of his mind's eye.

—AVL

Third Family Rectangle, 2022. Spanish cedar, spalted big leaf maple, avocado, Swiss pear, purple heart, cherry, loquat, black locust, hard maple, sapele, brass, and mother-of-pearl

Opposite: *Flowers Whisper to the Wind*, 2023. Hand-embroidered cotton on cotton

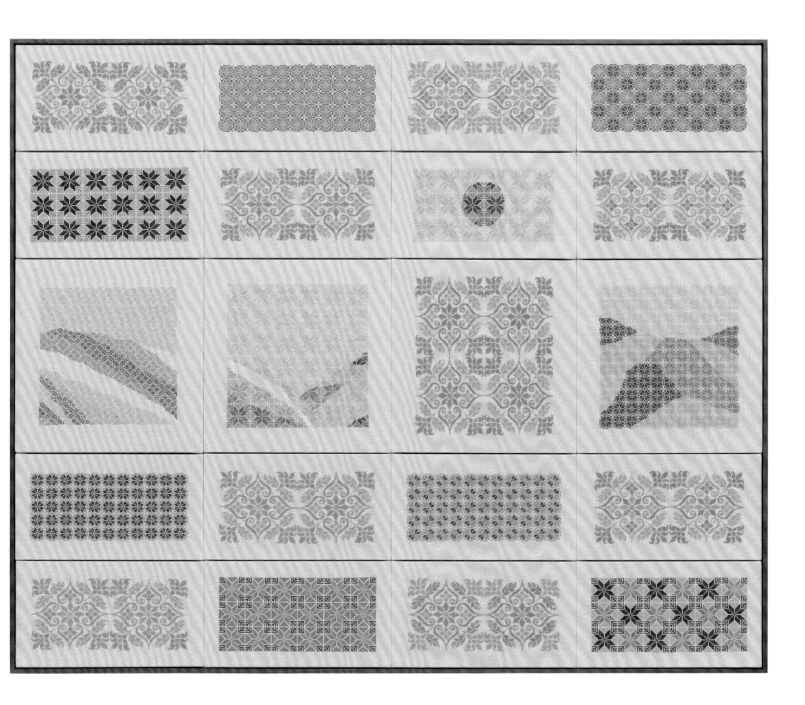

Installation view of *Jordan Nassar: Fantasy and Truth* at the Institute of Contemporary Art Boston, 2022–23

Opposite: Jordan Nassar in his studio, 2024

Coulter Fussell

B. 1977, Columbus, GA
Lives and works in Water Valley, MS
coulterfussell.com
@coulterfussell

Away from the hustle and bustle of metropolitan art hubs, Coulter Fussell has carved a place for herself in rural Mississippi to reimagine discarded materials into untraditional quilts. She combines bits and pieces donated to her studio into unexpected arrangements that reveal new narratives about motherhood and childhood nostalgia while honoring the histories embedded in the objects. Although a descendant of a long line of quilters, Fussell trained as a painter and only began quilting later in life by repurposing her old clothes, the most accessible and cheapest materials. Soon, people in town started dropping things off at her doorstep. With a self-imposed challenge to use everything that arrives democratically and without a hierarchy of value, her quilts have become more textural and sculptural over time to accommodate things like photographs, picture frames, ironing boards, and skateboard decks. Through her collaging practice, Fussell aims for material grafting, resulting in work that might look like a quilt or painting, but that is neither. In her trusted hands, the old becomes new, the lost is found, and castoffs are valuable again by extending the lives of material remnants as carriers of our stories.

—AVL

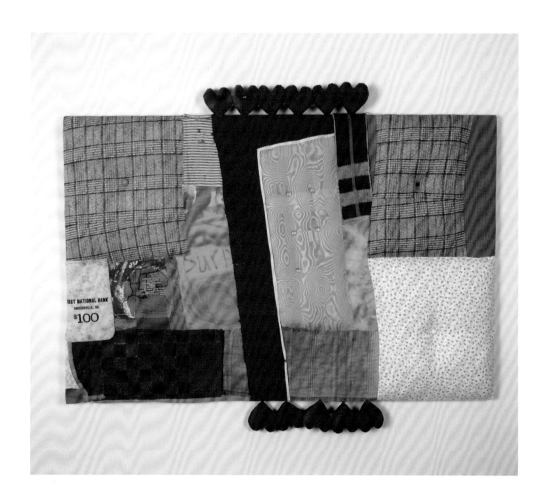

Heart Eyes, 2023. Donated textiles

Opposite: *Blue Skies*, 2023. Donated textiles

Florals, 2022. Donated textiles

Opposite, top: *Zero Bubble Submarine*, 2023.
Donated textiles, ironing board, and photographs

Bottom: Coulter Fussell's studio, 2023

Joyce J. Scott

B. 1948, Baltimore, MD
Lives and works in Baltimore, MD
@joycejscott

Joyce J. Scott's neckpieces are the epitome of statement jewelry. The virtuosic storyteller has shared impactful personal and political visual narratives for over four decades. A descendant of artists working in craft disciplines (including her mother, the renowned quilter and folk artist Elizabeth Talford Scott), the artist found her calling in the 1970s, working in glass. Although her practice spans many media, she is best known for her blown-glass sculptures and beaded jewelry, particularly her figurative neckpieces made using the Native American peyote stitch technique.

With a humble needle, thread, and thousands of tiny colorful glass beads, she weaves animated scenes that deliver big and bold messages about race, sex, gender, and American politics. She navigates a fine line between horror and humor to present charged yet subversive content to poke fun at stereotypes. Scott's work is dense with imagery, prompting a closer investigation of the realities of the human condition.

Her accolades include the American Craft Council Gold Medal for Consummate Craftsmanship (2020); honorary doctorates from the California College of the Arts, Maryland Institute College of Art, and Johns Hopkins University; the Smithsonian Visionary Award (2019); and a MacArthur Fellowship (2016).

—AVL

Bird Trapped in Shadows, 1981. Glass beads and thread. Rotasa Collection Trust

Opposite: *Mz. Teapot*, 2022. Glass beads, plastic beads, thread, wire, and armature

Top left: *Lovers*, 2005. Glass beads, thread, and tintypes. Collection of Karen Rotenberg

Right: *Mz. Teapot* (detail)

Opposite: *War, What is it Good For, Absolutely Nothin', Say it Again*, 2022. Glass beads and thread

Pauline Shaw

B. 1988, Kirkland, WA
Lives and works in Brooklyn, NY
@pauline___shaw

In 2015, Pauline Shaw learned she could make her own felt. This was a novel idea for the conceptual artist and an unexpected craft for someone with two art degrees in sculpture. Intrigued, she dove into online felting communities, often learning from women who had set up studios in the former bedrooms of their grown children. Shaw noticed that the touching, rubbing, and washing of raw wool was analogous to the feelings of nurture she experienced from her tutors. That tenderness could aid her quest to reconcile the discrepancy between considerable generational memories: her upbringing was spent between four countries, and for much of her life she believed her family to be Buddhist, discovering later they were Taoists. Was there any truth to her memories? To seek some sort of "proof," Shaw underwent MRI scans, "literally a picture that you get of the memory while you're thinking of it."[1] This data became visual confirmations whose patterns, topographies, and networks she abstracted through felting.

Shaw's pieces range from the size of posters to massive, suspended installations. They are the investment of time into tactile form and read as maps that shift from micro to macro, from brain waves to the cosmos. Some are combined with hand-blown glass orbs filled with tiny sculpture scapes of sugar and silver, reminiscent of domestic family altars. Of her tapestries, Shaw wants them to "occupy the same force that I think memory plays in our lives,"[2] however accurate it may be.

—KR

---

1 Pauline Shaw, interview by Kellie Riggs, July 25, 2023.
2 Shaw, interview.

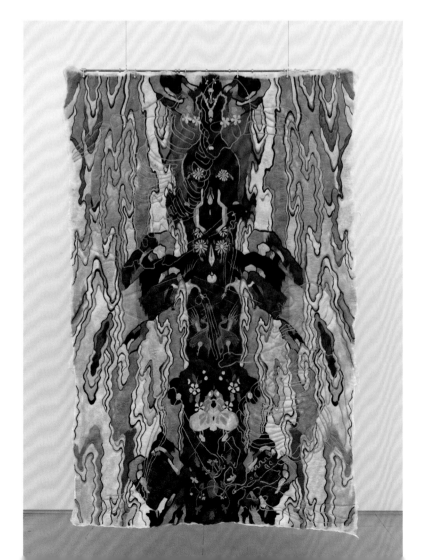

Knight Knight, 2023. Wool, silk, cotton scrim, and steel

Opposite: *Canopy*, 2023. Wool, silk, and cotton scrim

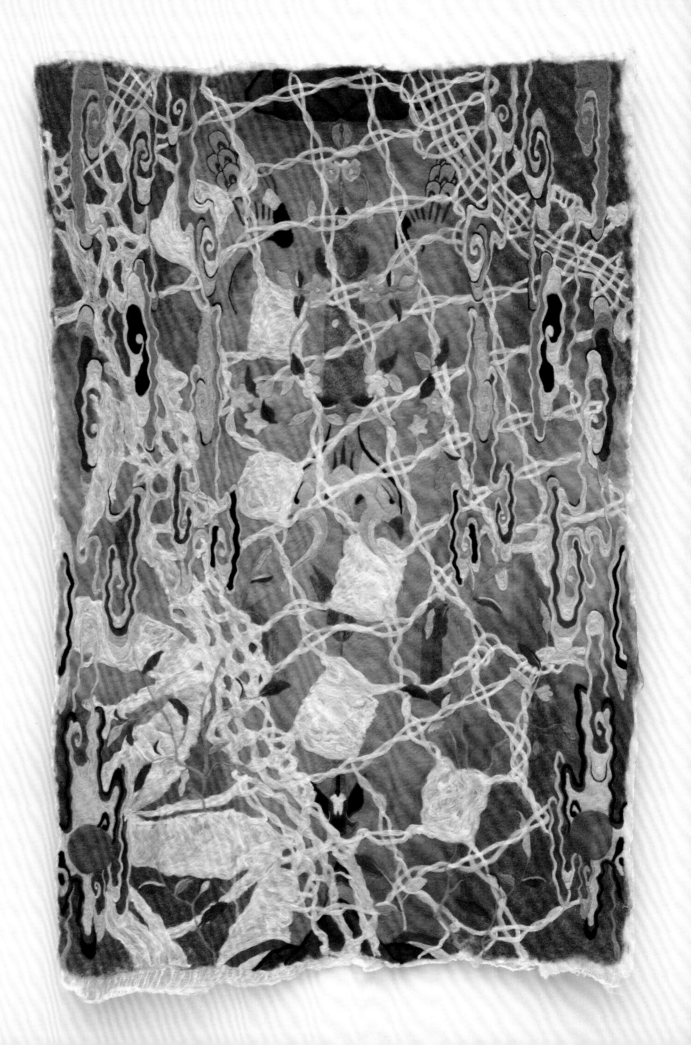

Opposite: *The Tombsweeper's Mosquito Bite*, 2021. Wool, silk, milk fiber, cotton gauze, pulley ballast system, glass weights with cast sugar, ash, joss paper, bronze, stone, silver, and water

Top left and right: *Flip Flop*, 2022. Glass, titanium dioxide, carved wood, silver chain, tiger's eye stone, paper, and steel hardware

Bottom, right: Pauline Shaw in her studio, 2023

Roberto Lugo

B. 1981, Philadelphia, PA
Lives and works in Wyncote, PA
robertolugostudio.com
@robertolugowithoutwax

In a 2021 interview for the *New York Times*, Roberto Lugo noted, "When I first started making ceramics, if anybody ever gave me a compliment, my joke was always 'Oh, you can go check out my work at the Met.'"[1] Since then, the artist has appeared in numerous exhibitions, but perhaps none more important than *Before Yesterday We Could Fly: An Afrofuturist Period Room* at the Metropolitan Museum of Art, where twenty-six of his works are on view in a room that celebrates a nonlinear storytelling tradition wedded in historical events, fantasy, and science fiction. Having the doors to one of the world's greatest museums open wide for him has liberated Lugo, and he is now telling personal stories in his work. His ongoing *Orange and Black* series, inspired by ancient Greek vessels, contains painful accounts

of his brother's incarceration and his childhood encounters with racism.

In his first solo show at R & Company, in 2023, Lugo constructed the Pigeon Crib, an homage to James McNeill Whistler's Peacock Room, featuring vessels with an encyclopedic fusion of patterns drawn from decorative arts history, from Rookwood tiles to Coogi sweaters. These works departed from Lugo's portraiture and narrative focus, focusing instead on iconography that represents both his family's agrarian past in Puerto Rico and his community in Philadelphia.

—JZ

1 Ted Loos, "His First Art Was Graffiti. Now His Pottery Is in the Met," *New York Times*, October 21, 2021, https://www.nytimes.com/2021/10/21/arts/roberto-lugo-ceramics.html.

Vessels from the *Conversation Piece* series, 2022. Glazed stoneware and luster

Opposite: *The Gilded Ghetto*, 2023. Glazed stoneware and enamel

Next pages, top left: *Gun Teapot: Rosa Parks*, 2021. Glazed ceramic, steel, epoxy, and enamel

Bottom: Roberto Lugo in his studio, 2023

Right: Installation view of *The Gilded Ghetto* at R & Company, 2023

Anina Major

B. 1981, Nassau, Bahamas
Lives and works in New York, NY, and Bennington, VT
aninamajor.com
@aninamajor

Anina Major tethers her sense of self and place between the United States and her homeland of the Bahamas through sculptures, installations, and performances that navigate the realities of diasporic life. She intertwines past, present, and future as she plaits the walls of her best-known work: ceramic vessels and sculptures resembling baskets. Major translates the straw-weaving techniques that many Bahamians, including her grandmother, have practiced to support their families for hundreds of years into clay. Tourist interest has historically supported straw craft in the Bahamas, but with a decrease in its demand by visitors to the islands, it is in peril of being forgotten.

Through clay, a material that has been key to the survival of artifacts and has shaped our understanding of human history, Major immortalizes the vulnerable tradition and recontextualizes the value of these crafts and the people who make them. She also underscores the disparity between leisure and labor depending on race, gender, and class within the tourist economy. Despite the distance, she is on a mission to underscore the fragility of history without stewardship while protecting and carrying forth a critical cultural inheritance on her own terms.

—AVL

Lush Mountaintop, 2023. Glazed stoneware and glass

Opposite: *Gathering Moss Beneath Nightsky*, 2023. Glazed stoneware, glass, and silver leaf

Installation view of *Inheritance* at Shoshana
Wayne Gallery, 2022

Opposite, clockwise from top left: *Lush
Mountaintop* (detail); *Gathering Moss Beneath
Nightsky* (detail); *Crowning Sunshine*, 2023.
Glazed stoneware, glass, gold leaf (detail)

B. 1997, Newton, MA
Lives and works in Boston, MA
nicoleamclaughlin.com
@nicole.a.mclaughlin

The cultivation and preservation of what Nicole McLaughlin feels is important to her identity is the foundation from which the ceramicist and fiber artist builds her practice. She has found a unique method to blend the two disciplines into a single object by embroidering the folding edges of glazed clay plates with hundreds of cascading hand-dyed threads. Her wall compositions seem to breathe their own life as they oscillate from hard to soft, taut to flowing. It is this fluidity between the two materials that reflects the transmission of the differing cultural aspects the artist experiences, who is first-generation Mexican American.

Whether it's emotional, cultural, or technical, every iteration of her work raises a new question grounded in self-discovery, and often they are linked to womanhood. As she says, "My grandmother, mother, and I have lived very different lives, three generations. Within that trajectory, tradition changes so much, and there are a lot of misunderstandings that happen with that."[1] McLaughlin's practice has thus been a familial bonding mechanism—one rich in symbolism related to motherhood, nourishment, and connection building—which she hopes continues in new ways as her position in the material lineage shifts. Having always made work from the perspective of being a daughter, what will happen when she becomes the mother of her very own?

—KR

1 Nicole McLaughlin, interview by Kellie Riggs, October 4, 2023.

Las Pequeñas, 2023. Terra-cotta, glaze, and cotton thread

Opposite: *La Corriente que nos Une*, 2021. Terra-cotta, glaze, Tencel, and natural indigo

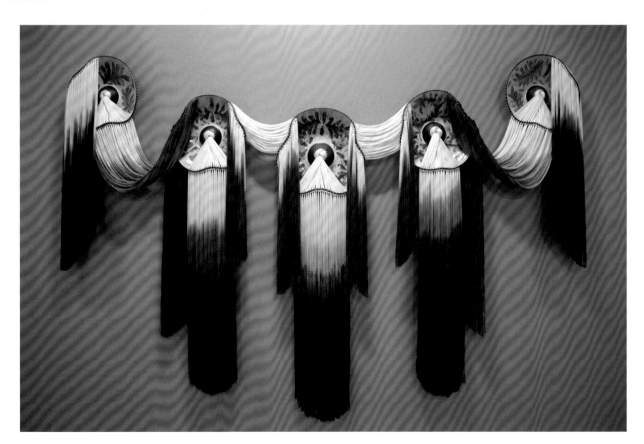

Opposite, top: *Rayo Mío; Mijo*, 2023. Terra-cotta, glaze, Tencel, cochineal dyed wool, and cotton

Bottom: *Sangre; Agua de Vida*, 2023. Terra-cotta, glaze, Tencel, and natural indigo

This page: Nicole McLaughlin in her studio, 2023

B. 1978, Juneau, AK
Lives and works in Phoenix, AZ
jamesjohnsonnativeart.com
@jamesjohnsonnativeart

For the last fifteen years, James Johnson has been perfecting his take on the ancient craft of Tlingit wood carving. He is self-taught and did not grow up within the culture of his people, the Tlingit Ch'áak' Dakl'aweidi Clan (Eagle Killerwhale), but has rectified this tenfold through his calling to pursue the traditional art form. To learn the foundations of formline—the term given to the particular style of Northwest Coast Indigenous art that utilizes fluid, curvilinear ovoids, U forms, and S forms—he looked to the past. Vigorous study of antique pieces in museum collections built the foundations for the artist, as did time with admired elders like Nathan Jackson, who encouraged compositional balance through drawing.

Johnson has become an inadvertent but passionate educator, constantly being invited to demonstrate his skills or speak about the art form at events; this openness has led to meaningful commercial collaborations. But it is the more traditional objects like clan hats that hold his attention most, carved from red or yellow cedar and inlaid with abalone. His renditions of seal bowls are often painted black to represent the historical grease bowls he studied, still dark and sticky centuries later. Though they bear his contemporary signature, it is important to Johnson that his pieces remain as functional as those used in ceremonies one thousand years ago, and one thousand years into the future.

—KR

Top: James Johnson on Tlingit Aani (also known as Juneau, AK), 2023

Right: *Tsaa x'ayeit (Seal Bowl)*, 2022. Red cedar and fish operculum

Opposite: *Gooch S'áaxwu (Wolf Headdress)*, 2023. Red cedar, abalone, horsehair, and wolf fur. Gochman Family Collection

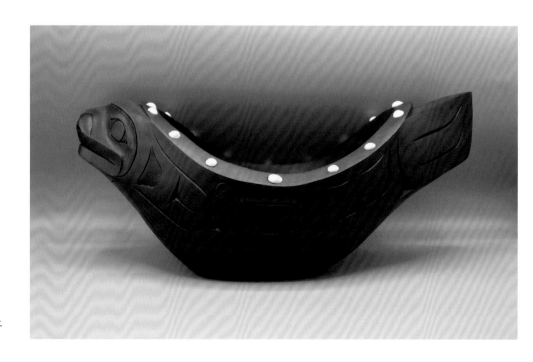

Clockwise from top left: James Johnson in his studio, 2023; *Kéet (Killerwhale)*, 2022. Skateboard deck. Volcom Collection; *Ch'áak dleit x̲ukat'áayi (Eagle Snowboard)*, 2018. Lib-Tech wood base; *Kudé kdagoot gaaw (Eclipse Drum)*, 2017. Deer hide

Opposite, top: *Xáat Heen (Salmon Stream)*, 2019. Mesquite wood

Bottom: *Ch'áak x'ayeit (Eagle Bowl)*, 2021. Yellow cedar and abalone

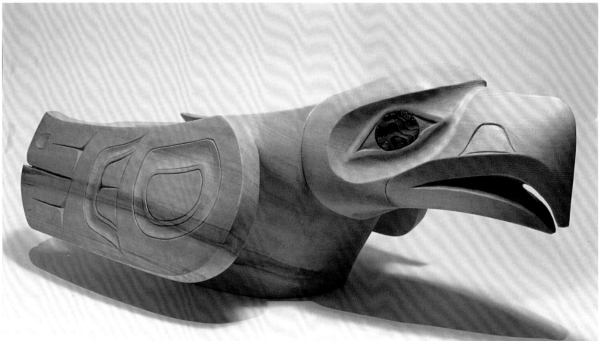

Venancio Aragon

B. 1985, Navajo Nation/Diné, Shiprock, NM
Lives and works in Farmington, NM
venancioaragon.com
@aragontextiles

In Venancio Aragon's rainbow tapestries, tradition and innovation become warp and weft. Navajo weaving is a technique that dates back hundreds of years, passed down from generation to generation. Aragon learned the skills from his mother, who is also a practicing weaver. He weaves technicolor compositions in a signature style he calls the "Expanded Rainbow Aesthetic," using an upright tension loom, a piece of ancient Indigenous technology. Through an untraditional polychromatic color palette consisting of over 250 synthetically and naturally hand-dyed yarn colors, bold geometric design, and an unrestrictive approach to expression, he experiments with techniques to preserve critical elements of his heritage while providing updates with his unique flare. Aragon also teaches the discipline to ensure the survival of this critical cultural tradition through a decolonized lens. Although he primarily makes experimental compositions, water and meteorological phenomena are often the subject matter of his work. His distorted or pixelated saturated tapestries thrive in the era of social media as they appear as if they are undergoing an optical illusion akin to digital glitches. The work proclaims Indigeneity in the present tense. Aragon's practice is, as he describes it, a "living record"[1] to carry his family's and community's legacy into the future.

—AVL

1 Venancio Aragon, "Artist Statement," Venancio Aragon, October 10, 2023, https://www.venancioaragon.com/artist-statement.html.

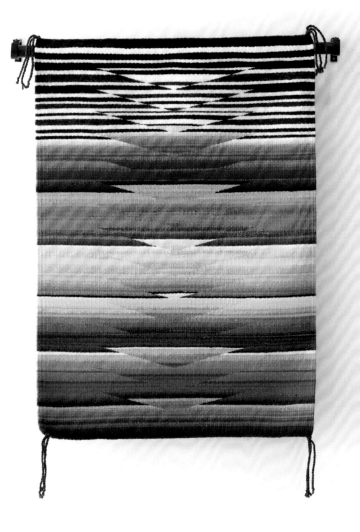

Rainbow Wedge, 2024. Wool, mohair, and dyes

Opposite: *Color Wave*, 2024. Wool, mohair, and dyes

Next pages: Venancio Aragon holding *Waiting for the Rain*, 2022. Wool, mohair, and dyes, on ancestral Pueblo and Navajo lands (also known as Angel Peak Scenic Area, NM), 2023

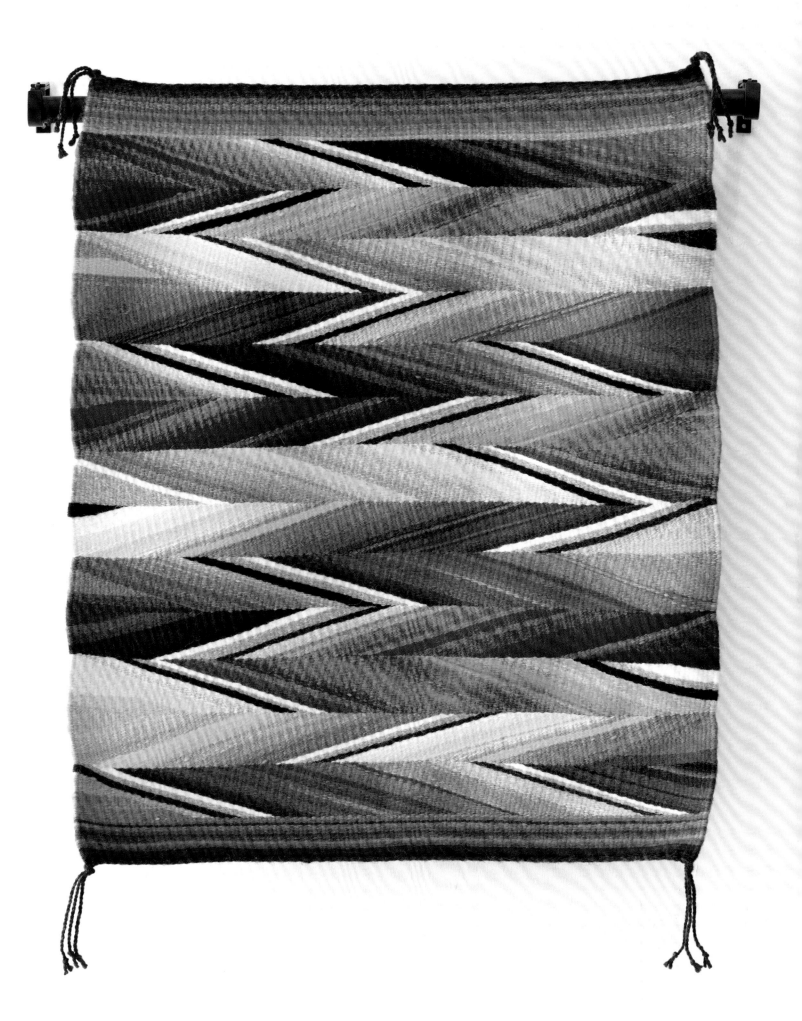

Glenn Adamson is a curator, writer, and historian based in New York and London. He has previously been director of the Museum of Arts and Design and head of research at the Victoria and Albert Museum. Dr. Adamson's publications include *Thinking Through Craft* (2007), *The Craft Reader* (2010), *Postmodernism: Style and Subversion* (2011, with Jane Pavitt), *The Invention of Craft* (2013), *Art in the Making* (2016, with Julia Bryan-Wilson), *Fewer Better Things: The Hidden Wisdom of Objects* (2018), *Objects: USA 2020*, and *Craft: An American History* (2021). His next book, *A Century of Tomorrows*, will be published by Bloomsbury in December 2024.

Zesty Meyers is the co-founder and principal of R & Company, which, for the past twenty-seven years, has established itself as one of the most prominent and groundbreaking design galleries in the world and has contributed to creating a renewed global interest in collectible design. Before R & Company, Meyers formed the radical installation and performance art group the B Team, which also later included R designer, Jeff Zimmerman, and R co-founder, Evan Snyderman. In 2016, Meyers contributed to the publication of *Brazil Modern: The Rediscovery of Twentieth-Century Brazilian Furniture*, the first internationally available inquiry into that country's richly significant design history.

Kellie Riggs is a curator and writer with a background in art jewelry and craft-based processes. Projects include designer Misha Kahn's first solo museum show, *Under the Wobble Moon, Objects from the Capricious Age*, at Villa Stuck in Munich, Germany (2022), and *Non-Stick Nostalgia: Y2K Retrofuturism in Contemporary Jewelry* at the Museum of Arts and Design (2019). Riggs is also the creator of the reoccurring artist-run exhibition *FOTOCOPY*, which since 2018 has had editions in Munich, New York, Venice, and Amsterdam. As a writer and editor, Riggs has contributed to various national and international publications over the past ten years, including as editor for *Current Obsession*.

Evan Snyderman founded the gallery R 20th Century (now R & Company) with Zesty Meyers, which has since established itself as one of the most prominent design galleries in the world, with Snyderman as the creative and artistic director. Snyderman has contributed to multiple publications since 2000, including monographs on Wendell Castle, Greta Magnusson Grossman, Poul Kjaerholm, Renate Müller, Verner Panton, Ilmari Tapiovaara, Jeff Zimmerman, David Wiseman, and Rogan Gregory, as well as overviews on Italian Radical design and American craft and design. In 2023, Snyderman and Meyers received the Iris Award for Outstanding Dealer, honoring their contributions to design and the decorative arts.

Angelik Vizcarrondo-Laboy is a curator and writer advocating for underrepresented communities, stories, materials, and approaches in the art world. She has curated and juried exhibitions across the United States, including at the Crocker Art Museum, Mindy Solomon Gallery, the Center for Craft, and the critically acclaimed *Funk You Too! Humor and Irreverence in Ceramic Sculpture* at the Museum of Arts and Design (2023). Vizcarrondo-Laboy has written for many publications. Her new book, *New Women's Work*, with Smith Street Books, is slated for 2024. Vizcarrondo-Laboy also co-created and co-hosts the podcast *Clay in Color*, celebrating some of the brightest emerging and established voices working with clay from the global majority.

CREDITS

© Adam Grinovich: 98 (bottom), 99, 100, 101; photo by Rob Chron: 98 (top)
© Almine Rech: 112 (bottom), 113 (left)
© Amia Yokoyama: 120–21 (center); photo by Jonathan Chacon: 118 (top)
© Anina Major, photo by Andrew White: 250 (bottom), 251, 253; photo by Melissa Alcena: 250 (top)
© Anne Libby, photo by Kyle Knodell: 158 (top)
© Ashes/Ashes: 81 (right)
© Astitva Singh & Ricardo Vaz: 88
© Brian Oakes: 25 (left), 94, 95, 96; photo by Joey Frank: 97
© Cammie Staros, photo by Juliana Paciulli: 130 (top)
© Carl D'Alvia: 168; photo by Charles Benton: 166 (top); photo by Joerg Lohse: 169 (top)
© Chen Chen & Kai Williams: 126; photo by Siggy Bodolai: 128
© Collection of Karen Rotenberg, photo by Jordan Robles: 240 (left)
© Collin Leitch: 155, 156 (top); photo by Izzy Leung: 154, 156 (bottom left); photo by Jason Mandella: 156 (bottom right), 157
© Coulter Fussell: 234, 235, 236, 237
© Culture Object and Trey Jones: 217; photo by Donovan Gerald: 214 (top), 216; photo by Jody Kivort: 214 (bottom), 215
© Dallas Museum of Art, TWO x TWO for AIDS, and Art Fund for Wearable Art, photo by Mallory Weston: 82 (bottom)
© David B. Smith Gallery and Justin Favela, photo by Mikayla Whitmore: 195
© Dee Clements: 201 (bottom); photo by Evan Jenkins: 198 (top)
© Embajada Gallery: 106 (bottom)
© Eric Swanson: 58 (top)
© FOX & WILDS / Marina Makropoulos: 35
© Francesca DiMattio: 142 (top)
© Friedman Benda and Misha Kahn: 206 (top); photo by Andreas Zimmermann: 207 (bottom); photo by PEPE fotografia: 206 (bottom), 208–9; photo by Sean Davidson: 36 (top); photo by Timothy Doyon: 207 (top)
© Gardens by the Bay: 22 (top)
© Georgina Treviño: 107, 108; photo by Maxine Alo: 106 (top)
© Gochman Family Collection, photo by Alon Koppel: 259
© HESSE FLATOW and Carl D'Alvia: 169 (bottom); photo by Charles Benton: 30, 166 (bottom); photo by Jenny Gorman: 167
© Houston Center for Contemporary Craft, photo by Katy Anderson: 102 (bottom), 103, 105 (bottom)
© Hugh Hayden: 174 (top)
© James Cohan, Anat Ebgi, The Third Line, and Jordan Nassar, photo by Dan Bradica: 231; photo by Matthew Kroening: 230 (bottom)
© James Johnson: 258 (bottom), 260 (top right), 261 (bottom); photo by Ian Tetzner: 41 (top), 260 (top left, bottom left, bottom right), 261 (top); photo by Scott Baxter: 258 (top)
© Jamie Bennett: 70 (top), 72

© Jason McDonald: 186 (top), 187; photo by German Vasquez: 186 (bottom), 188 (left), 189; photo by Krista May: 188 (right)
© John D. and Catherine T. MacArthur Foundation: 238 (top)
© Jolie Ngo, photo by Evan Soroka: 74 (top)
© Jordan Nassar, photo by Andy Jackson: 230 (top); photo by Timothy O'Connell: 233
© Joshua Franzos: 246 (top)
© Joyce Lin: 21 (left), 90 (top), 92 (top left, top right, bottom left)
© Justin Favela and Petersen Automotive Museum: 34
© Justin Favela, photo by Krystal Ramirez: 194 (bottom); photo by Michal Palma: 196–97; photo by Mikayla Whitmore: 194 (top)
© Katie Stout: 152 (bottom); photo by Alex Trebus: 150 (top); photo by Blaine Davis: 151, 152 (top)
© Kohler Co.: 32, 178 (bottom), 180 (top left)
© la BEAST: 110 (bottom)
© Layla Klinger: 25 (right); photo by Elisheva Gavra: 102 (top), 105 (top)
© Liam Lee: 162, 163, 164, 165
© Lilah Rose: 110 (top), 111, 112 (top), 113 (right)
© Linda Nguyen Lopez: 172 (bottom left); photo by Mark Jackson: 171, 172 (right), 173; photo by Meredith Mashburn: 170 (top)
© Lisson Gallery and Hugh Hayden: 174 (bottom), 175, 176–77
© Magenta Plains and Anne Libby: 158 (bottom), 161 (top and bottom right); photo by Object Studies: 160–61
© Mahnaz Collection, photo by Hee Jin Kang: 37, 218 (bottom), 219, 220 (right), 221; photo by Jared Chavez: 218 (top), 220 (left top to bottom)
© Mallory Weston: 83
© Marta Gallery and Minjae Kim, photo by Erik Benjamins: 54 (bottom)
© Mary Lee Hu: 64 (bottom); photo by Doug Yaple: 62 (top)
© Matt McKnight / Reuters Pictures: 24 (top)
© Matthew Szösz: 89 (top); photo by Alex Miller: 89 (bottom); photo by James Harnois: 86; photo by Mark Johnston: 87
© Mindy Solomon Gallery: 170 (bottom); photo by Brandon Forrest Frederick: 172 (top left)
© Minjae Kim, photo by Dominik Tarabanski: 56; photo by Jesper Lund: 54 (top)
© MJ Tyson: 134
© Mobilia Gallery and Mary Lee Hu, photo by Daniel Fox: 63; photo by Doug Yaple: 64 (top), 65; photo by Richard Nicol: 62 (bottom)
© Mobilia Gallery, photo by Michael Koryta: 239, 240 (right), 241
© Mtdozier23 / Dreamstime: 42
© Museum of American Glass at WheatonArts: 21 (right)
© Museum of Arts and Design, photo by John Bigelow Taylor: 39
© Museum Villa Stuck, photo by Nina Moog: 36 (bottom)
© Myra Mimlitsch-Gray: 138 (bottom), 141 (bottom); photo by Christopher Preis: 138 (top), 139; photo by Ken Gray: 140 (top)

ACKNOWLEDGMENTS

Thank you to all participating artists for your inspiring work, which made this project possible.

We are grateful to the following institutions and individuals for their expertise and assistance:
Culture Object
David B. Smith Gallery
Friedman Benda
Goya Contemporary Gallery
HESSE FLATOW
James Cohan
Karen Rotenberg
Magenta Plains
Mahnaz Collection
Mobilia Gallery
Nancy Margolis Gallery
Nazarian / Curcio
Nina Johnson
Sienna Patti Contemporary
Superhouse
The American Museum of Ceramic Art
The Future Perfect
The Museum of Arts and Design

Special thanks to:
Dung Ngo
Elizabeth Smith
Phil Kovacevich
and the R & Company staff.

First published in the United States of
America in 2024 by
August Editions
and
R & Company

Library of Congress Control Number:
2024909274

ISBN: 978-1-947359-13-0

Design by Phil Kovacevich

First edition

Printed in China